James Allanson Picton

**New theories and the old faith**

A course of lectures on religious topiecs of the day

James Allanson Picton

**New theories and the old faith**

*A course of lectures on religious topiecs of the day*

ISBN/EAN: 9783337131760

Printed in Europe, USA, Canada, Australia, Japan

Cover: Foto ©Lupo / pixelio.de

More available books at **www.hansebooks.com**

# NEW THEORIES AND THE OLD FAITH.

A COURSE OF LECTURES ON

RELIGIOUS TOPICS OF THE DAY,

DELIVERED IN

ST. THOMAS'S SQUARE CHAPEL, HACKNEY,

BY THE

REV. J. ALLANSON PICTON, M.A.

WILLIAMS AND NORGATE,
14, HENRIETTA STREET, COVENT GARDEN, LONDON;
AND 20, SOUTH FREDERIC STREET, EDINBURGH.
1870.

BLEACH AND DEARLING,
PRINTERS,
BISHOPSGATE WITHOUT, E.C.

## NOTICE.

THOSE readers who were also hearers of the following Course of Lectures will observe that it has been increased by the addition of the first discourse, which was preached earlier in the year. The purpose of that sermon seemed to fall in with the general aims of the succeeding course so well that it was difficult to resist the temptation to include it, though it is to be feared that here and there the similarity amounts to repetition. The compression and occasional mutilation caused by limits of time has been in some places repaired by expansion; but the comparative freedom—perhaps roughness—of oral delivery is preserved.

## LECTURE I.

|                                                               | PAGE |
| ------------------------------------------------------------- | ---- |
| THE SOUL'S LONGING AFTER A FINAL CAUSE                        | 1    |

## LECTURE II.

THE GOD-CONSCIOUSNESS IN HUMANITY . . . 31

## LECTURE III.

INSPIRATION . . . . . 69

## LECTURE IV.

INFALLIBILITY . 104

## LECTURE V.

THE USE AND ABUSE OF THE BIBLE . . 140

## APPENDIX.

Note A.—ON BUDDHISM AS AN ARGUMENT FOR THE POSSI-
BILITY OF REST IN ATHEISM . . . . 185
B.—ON THE DEVELOPMENT THEORY IN RELATION TO
THE SOUL AND IMMORTALITY . . . 190
C.—ON NATURAL PROCESS AND ORIGINAL FORCE . . 204
„ D.—ON THE METAPHYSICAL ISSUES OF PHYSICAL
SCIENCE . . . . . 207
E.—ON ST. PAUL'S REVELATIONS 209
F. EUSEBIUS ON THE CANON . 219
G. ON THE DIVINITY OF CHRIST 223

# LECTURE I.

## THE SOUL'S LONGING AFTER A FINAL CAUSE.

*"The eye is not satisfied with seeing, nor the ear filled with hearing."*—Eccl. i. 8.

*"That they should seek the Lord, if haply they might feel after Him and find Him."*—Acts xvii. 27.

IF, as I presume, you all take an interest in the progress of scientific discovery and the consequent modifications in theological opinion during the last half-century, I cannot appeal to unsympathetic hearts when I say that sometimes the future seems a very dreary outlook. I do not of course refer to the revolutions in time-honoured organizations and modes of thought, which appear more and more inevitable. The issue with which I propose to deal is much deeper than that. A vapour "heavy, hueless, formless, cold" creeps more and more above the distant horizon, and we feel as though its touch must be so far deadlier than physical death, that we would very much rather die before it comes any nearer. In one word, as all our bodily actions tend to death, so, to some moods of mind at the present day, all activities of thought seem to have but one inevitable goal, a blank material atheism. I am of course not stating my own fears; though I should be ill prepared to deal with the subject if I had never felt them. But I can easily understand the frame of mind to which in view of prevalent currents of thought at the present day, it may appear that there is no ultimate issue possible other than the one I have named. Let us therefore at the outset put the fears natural to such a frame of mind in the most plausible light, in order that we may not overestimate our resources against them.

The tendencies of the future, it may be urged, are to be augured, not from the present enthusiasms or prejudices of the many, but rather from the uniform leanings of those leaders of thought, who best know what the significance of scientific progress is. Indeed the real state of public opinion now is to be gathered, not from formulas of religious profession or worship, but rather from the practical attitude of men's minds, and the conclusions which this tacitly assumes. Judging then in this way of the general tendency of thought, we may regard certain positions as permanently and irreversibly taken up, at least by the sort of minority which always decides the future of the world. It used to be regarded as a great stretch of charity if one could hope for the salvation of a Romanist or a Unitarian. But now it has come practically to this, that no intellectual opinion whatever whether religious or otherwise can possibly save or condemn a man's soul. We are simply to apply the rule "by their fruits ye shall know them" impartially to Atheists, Deists and Christians, making abstraction altogether of their opinions while we do so. Farther, no one can now state a theory of the infallibility of the Bible, without encumbering it with so many limitations as to amount practically to its denial. Again the unmistakeable and, it may be added the resistless tendency of science is to extend the reign of law not only to all phenomena of existing nature, but also to every conceivable process in its development. And still farther, physiologists exhibit an always increasing confidence that all movements of mind are associated with, and find their equivalent expression in changes in the matter of the brain. What more is needed, ask some, to show that atheism is already clearly in view? One by one all sacred principles and objects of reverence are undermined or exploded: and very soon we shall have nothing left to us beyond what we can touch and taste and handle,—matter, nothing but matter, godless matter, or in other words material atheism.

I might reply, I am not so sure of that, at least so far as concerns the issue. Why should matter necessarily be godless? To urge that conclusion so confidently one ought to have found out what matter is; and I am not aware that any one has done so yet. The most plausible conjectures on the subject would rather begin an upward movement in the everlasting see-saw of opinion, by showing that matter is only a form of force, or aggregation of forces. And this would certainly point the way back to spiritualism. No; I am not at all sure that the reduction of everything to matter would involve atheism: in fact rather the contrary. As in Browning's famous ring, the base alloy needed to work out the theory would fly off on its completion, and leave only forces, which, if they inhere in anything, are more likely to inhere in spirit and life than in aught else.

But that is scarcely the kind of reply to the religious fears of the times which I desire to urge now. I wish rather to insist on a principle in human nature which really makes the issue of all such controversies a fore-gone conclusion, however perplexing and uncertain they may appear to be in their course. A traveller, who comes upon a winding river in an unknown mountainous land, is not more sure that the ultimate destiny of that river is the sea, than we may be about the final issue of the *only* controversy which can be regarded as a question of spiritual life or death. I do not for a moment deny that individual men may conscientiously hold atheistic opinions. But I say that to regard these instances as prophetic tokens of the final destiny of human thought is just as though, standing by a river and noticing a back eddy here and there, you were to fancy that at some point in its course the stream might turn round and go up hill. In both cases there is an inward principle which, in spite of apparent exceptions to its working, all explicable on close examination, points to one only possible ultimate issue. In a word, what gravitation is to the stream, that I contend, the irrepressible longing of the soul after a final cause of existence is to the course of human opinion. It makes atheism for ever impossible, unless as a very exceptional position, and then only provisional, the negative expedient of suspense, not the confidence of assurance. Of course the position is not self-evident; and therefore the first thing that we have to do is to explain and support it. Afterwards I shall ask your attention to the degrees and disguises of which the apprehension of this final cause is susceptible, and the security which we have for its ultimate achievement in ourselves and others.

I.

This, says St. Paul, is the reason why God made the world; that it might be the abode of men, and that they might seek the Lord. We cannot help asking ourselves how comes St. Paul to speak with such confidence of God's object in the creation of mankind? To say that he does so by inspiration is to say little, because the term, though, as we shall try to show in another lecture, it has a very real significance, is so exceedingly indefinite. Is this a part of the information he received in the ecstatic visions of his exalted intercourse with the risen Lord? That does not appear likely, for this reason: that all St. Paul's references to this source of his knowledge seem to imply that the instructions he thus received concerned only the special form in which he, as the Apostle of the Gentiles, was to preach the gospel. Did he learn it from the Old Testament? Well, it is implied in the Old Testament; but in such a mode that perhaps only those who bring this idea to the study of its pages are likely to find it there. I rather think that St. Paul in these words uttered a truth, which he in his consciousness found fundamentally necessary, while it was doubtless illustrated and developed by his Christian experience. Indeed the whole tone of the speech on Mars' Hill is that of one who desires to appeal to first principles. He speaks not as a Jew, but as a man. And he was a man who could not take life easily. He could not live, as the saying is, from hand to mouth. There are some men who appear satisfied with the consciousness that they are alive, and are on the whole enjoying it. But not such a man was St. Paul. He felt driven to seek for some ulterior significance in life, some divine purpose, attainment of which should be the highest goal and perfect bliss of man. And this instinctive impulse found, as he believed, its explanation and its satisfaction in the divine life which Christ awoke in his soul and was awaking in the world. Therefore he says with such confidence that the Most High has made all nations of men that they should seek the Lord. Now this is inspiration undoubtedly; but it is an inspiration which is open to us all, and which in some degree we all possess, whether we yield to it or not; for it is just the quenchless longing of human nature after a final cause of creation.

These remarks upon St. Paul's words may illustrate the meaning that we are to attach to the phrase 'final cause,' in this connection. I mean by it such a supreme and comprehensive motive, or purpose, as would give us a rational if only approximate conception of the ultimate significance of creation. Of course our observations are necessarily confined to the part of creation in which humanity is unmistakeably the predominant feature. But whatever satisfies the craving for a final cause here will also suggest the possibility of an analogous motive pervading the whole universe.

Let no one think that because science has no place for final causes therefore there is no place for them in philosophy or religion. As an anatomist, or a botanist, or a geologist, the student may be very right in saying, I have nothing to do with final causes, my only business is with observed appearances and ascertained connections. But as a *man* he cannot help himself; final causes will obtrude upon him whether he likes it or not. For as a man he not only sees and classifies, but he wistfully thinks and wonders. There are relations between himself and the universe, which no analysis of sensuous observations can exhaust. The starry sky has some nameless grandeur, which no results of mathematical calculation can express. The tender clouds, whose colours he analyses with his prism, speak a language to his heart, which no prismatic chart can interpret. And amongst such incalculable relations between himself and the universe is the wistful longing after inner meaning and ultimate aim, which the enigma of creation always excites in the contemplative soul. Most natural is the artless hymn which represents the young child as appealing to the little star on high and exclaiming, "How I wonder what you are!" So all life long we stand at gaze, the vision expanding from a star to a universe, while still all our cry is of wonder what it is. And this enquiry after what *is*, includes manifestly a longing after the significance and purpose of appearances; that is, it involves the hunger of the soul for a final cause of creation.

But it is time to show the relation of this to the moral and religious outlook of the age. For, as we have said, the fear is entertained by many, that critical, physiological, and philosophical enquiries all converge on one inevitable goal—Atheism. Well then let us suppose the goal to be reached. Let us imagine the Bible to be regarded, not only as fallible, but as delusive, and God to be given up as a poetic myth. Let us conceive the reign of law so interpreted as to exclude any possible freedom of will; let us assume it established as the combined triumph of all scientific enquiries, that in every direction the last obtainable result leaves us with centres of force and their vibrations. Does any one think that such a conclusion can ever be regarded as shutting up the mysteries of the universe or closing the avenues of spiritual perspective? Opinions change, but human nature survives; and no decrees of a scientific hierarchy can long hush the questions, what is force, or how is it gathered into centres, and why do they for ever vibrate, and what is the stupendous movement working out? If there is a balance of forces in the universe, why do they not neutralize one another? If there is not, how are we held off from chaos? And is there no meaning in it all, no purpose accordant with mind and heart and conscience in man? Is the universe but a stupendous kaleidoscope, in which forms of beauty tumble together, only to be scattered by the next revolution? If it be so, I am not of that world on which I look through the window of the eye. In this etherial inward world to which I belong, will, purpose, reason, affection, principle reign as supreme all-animating powers. And I, being as I am, have no part nor lot in that great and terrible wilderness masked with a shimmering mirage of beauty that rings me round. Nay, I am myself more real than anything without. That desert world is a dream for aught I know; but as for me I *live*—and Oh for a universal life, that in it I may live and move and have my being! Surely, surely they were right of old who said that life was the beginning and the end of all. And what if after all the forces of which men speak and their vibrations be the signs of some eternal energy of life?

" The sun, the moon, the stars, the seas, the hills and the plains,
Are not these, O soul, the vision of Him who reigns?
Is not the vision He? though he be not that which He seems?

Dreams are true while they last, and do we not live in dreams?
Speak to Him thou, for He hears, and spirit with spirit can meet,
Closer is He than breathing, and nearer than hands and feet."

But it will not need modern poets to give voice to the resurrection joy of faith. There was one of old who to a Hebrew harp uttered words, which may yet express the repentance of a world awaking from a short nightmare of material atheism. "*So foolish was I and ignorant, I was as a beast before thee. Nevertheless I am continually with thee; thou hast holden me by my right hand. Thou shalt guide with thy counsel, and afterward receive me to glory. Whom have I in heaven but thee? And there is none upon earth that I desire beside thee. My flesh and my heart faileth, but God is the strength of my heart and my portion for ever.*"

I believe then this irrepressible longing after a final cause, after some significance and purpose in creation, which shall have due reference to human nature, will for ever make atheism impossible except as a temporary expedient of suspense, or the paralysis of despair which comes in the darkest hours of times transitional through decay.\* For human nature is a part of the universe, and in interpreting the universe it must surely have due weight. If then the hunger after a final cause be as ineradicable from fully developed human nature as the belief itself that the senses really imply an external world, I regard it as a very important indication

\* See Appendix Note A on Buddhism as an argument for the possibility of rest in Atheism.

that a final cause exists. I do not now say how far it can come into clear consciousness. I do not contend that it can ever be adequately and absolutely apprehended. But I do say that it may hint itself to the spiritual imagination. I do contend that it may give prophetic types of its reality in the noblest moments of this mortal life, as the glory of manly or womanly love may be anticipated in the affections of the child. And if immortality should be the ever growing apprehension of this final cause, that itself is sufficient to make heaven an exhaustless joy, a joy which continually enlarges the power of perception, and for ever exceeds its capacity.

The suggestion which St. Paul makes as to the nature of the final cause of creation is this, that the world was evolved for the purpose of bringing about the communion of the created spirit with the eternal God. The value of this suggestion will be better understood, when we have considered the degrees and disguises of which that communion is susceptible. Meantime I urge that, like truth and love, this is one of those things which commend themselves to our spiritual perceptions as good and worthy for their own sakes, apart from any other considerations whatever. Nay, every special instance of our joy in truth and love suggests a larger range of such bliss; nor can the imagination once aroused stop short of a possible universe, in which every creature is blessed because consciously true to the divine thought, consciously embraced by and responsive to the divine love. In such a conception, and in such a conception only can we find an ultimate rest for our souls. Give us that, and we find no insuperable difficulty in the long, slow, often painful process of development which leads up to the final issue. For it may well be that degrees and contrasts of finite experience are necessary to the fulness of that issue, and when enshrined therein will explain themselves. Give us that, and it is not even needful for us to imagine that creation, development, conflict, redemption shall ever really cease. A completed universe, a closed heaven, an exhausted mystery may be only an expedient of the mind for facility in embodying the desires of the heart. But those desires in their essential significance are satisfied, if we can dare to conceive of some pinnacle in the throne of God, from which the universe though in eternal flux, is seen to be working out in every newly created part some fresh creature consciousness of the Divine Life.

Though no such comprehensive vision be possible to us now, still there are many hints that the purest and keenest happiness which existence ever yields us is of the nature of communion with God. When we indignantly revolt from wrong and earnestly stand up for right, the impulse which sustains us is felt to be a triumphant joy. And I know not better how to describe that impulse than by the word loyalty—loyalty to the Supreme Goodness which all in one sense or another, however dimly, feel to be the ultimate law of existence. And in the warmth of this loyalty I recognise the embrace of our souls by God's purity and love. The very eagerness of science in the pursuit of natural truth receives in my view its real explanation, only when we think of each new discovery as a fresh hint of the eternal light in which all things are open and unconcealed to the consciousness of God. And when the Psalmist in his own rapture at the magnificence of the world aspires to think of the bliss of the Creator in His work—"*the glory of the LORD shall endure for ever, the LORD shall rejoice in his works*"—I think he suggests the real secret of the strange and deep emotions which are stirred in our hearts by our intercourse with Nature. When we can stand in the midst of God's beautiful universe, and feel that we love it because He loves it, and that our love is one with His; when we can realize it as living because He lives, nay as being only the transparent veil that moderates His intolerable light: then we know why every feature of noble scenery has a meaning to the soul as well as to the eye. For our hearts are not alone in the universe; they answer through the veil to the life of God. Then we know why the purity of Alpine peaks should touch the heart with aspiration; and why the sweet perspective of a woodland glade should dim the eyes with tears; and why the ocean murmurs of eternity; and why all sounds of nature seem to wail or sigh, with longing more than sadness. For what is love in God is longing in his creatures. "*As for me I will behold thy face in righteousness. I shall be satisfied when I awake with thy likeness.*"

*"The earnest expectation of the creature waiteth for the manifestation of the sons of God."*

## II.

It will naturally occur to many that if the final cause of creation be the communion of the creature with the creator, there is, at any rate so far as the field of human observation extends, hardly any conceivable end which creation has hitherto fulfilled so little. But such a thought is probably suggested by too limited an idea of the meaning of communion between the Creator and the creature. To this limited idea consciousness on the part of the creature that it is God to whom the heart answers is considered absolutely necessary. Now that is true no doubt of the highest communion. But if God gives himself in some measure to all His creatures, and if their feelings are anything to Him, then there may be endless degrees and disguises of this communion; or the final cause of creation may be attained more or less perfectly, and in many ways. The meaning of this will perhaps become clearer as we proceed. But first of all it must be plain that by the attainment of the final cause of creation in any single instance we cannot mean only an intellectual apprehension of it. What we mean is such a practical realization as satisfies the desires of the soul. For example, my opinion as to this final cause might be held with intellectual clearness, even while in tone and temper and deeds I might be selfish, base and false, that is, utterly ungodly. But in such a case it could not for one moment be maintained that in me the ultimate aim of creation was realized. Yet though my intellectual notions on the subject might be considered imperfect, still, if in my soul I realize anything of the tone and temper which come from communion with God, and if I am the means of infusing something of this spirit into those about me, then the end of creation is to that extent attained in me; and I am made the instrument of promoting it in others. This remark is obvious enough; but it leads us a good deal farther. For if an intellectual apprehension of the final cause of creation is nothing apart from the life that shows a moral communion with God, the question naturally arises, supposing the life to exist altogether apart from any correct intellectual apprehension of its source, what then? Does the absence of a right opinion change the essential nature of the life? The answer may be ready on many lips, that such a case is impossible. But some of our greatest perplexities at the present time arise from the practical proof to the contrary, which is forced on us by all social experience except the narrowest and most sectarian. And nothing but a forlorn or perverse determination to construe the most unconformable facts according to a preconceived theory can long maintain such an answer. The smallest circle of society, containing any marked varieties of thought and character, is quite sufficient to illustrate the startling and paradoxical extent to which moral and spiritual life is independent of theological opinion. To bring the argument to a point, take an extreme case, which unfortunately is too common at the present day. It is by no means uncommon to meet with men not only of keen activity of thought, but of high purpose and chivalrous temper, who, when pressed, will tell you that we do not and cannot know whether there is a God at all, and that at all events any personal direct and conscious communion with Him is impossible. Yet often the life of such men, not the outward semblance only, but the essential character, so far as the most intimate intercourse can ascertain it, is distinguished by uprightness, kindliness, earnestness, loyalty of soul, sometimes even by the enthusiasm from which self-forgetfulness and self-sacrifice are inseparable. Now there, as a matter of fact, you have the life without the opinion. Well, will any one undertake to say that the final cause of creation is to *no* extent realized in such cases? Are uprightness, truth, honour and love any the less divine because the intellect of their possessor is mistaken about their fundamental nature and origin? You might just as well deny that they are spiritual at all, because their possessor's theory is that they are functions of the tissue of his brain. Our creation by the hand of God does not depend upon our opinion on the question. And the procession of all good thoughts and holy desires from the Spirit of the Most High is just as much a question of fact; and therefore surely independent of the opinions of those in whom good thoughts and holy desires are awakened.

At the same time truth or falsehood of opinion is never indifferent, least of all on subjects of such transcendant import. For in the unity of our personal being our faculties are to such an extent mutually interdependent, that the opinions to which we have alluded, though they cannot affect the essential nature of the moral life, must of course prevent its highest development as a clear consciousness of God in the soul. The *God-consciousness* indeed is, as I shall try to show in another lecture, itself capable of many degrees, and in its obscurer forms may co-exist with the most erroneous, even with materialistic opinions. But to become a *consciousness of God*, it necessarily demands—or perhaps in becoming this it produces—an intellectual apprehension of the filial relations between ourselves and the Father in Heaven. I can well believe that the full attainment of our ideal perfection is the co-ordinate result of accuracy in opinion and loyalty in heart. But I cannot and dare not believe that in any individual man the final cause of his creation is wholly missed because, in the candid exercise of his reason, he arrives at erroneous opinions even as to the being of God. Nor can I deny that such instances of candid conscientious though as I am very sure fundamental error exist, without doing violence, I will not say to charity, but to common sense. Yet in the scope for unwarped judgement which the frank acceptance of such a position gives me I am, if possible, more confident than ever that conscious communion with God is open to all seeking souls, and must needs be a nobler state and a keener joy than any blind participation in his life. For he who can trace the mystic light that conscience loves, who can follow it up the beams of heaven and find its source in the brightness of God's glory is more consistent, and is likely to be more earnest, in cherishing that light with reverence, than any man who finds in it only an electric condition of the brain. All I contend is that the one opinion or the other cannot possibly alter the essential nature of the moral life, and therefore cannot change its character as a communion with God.

The use of this word communion to express anything short of personal conscious and recognized relationship to God will no doubt appear incongruous to some. Yet, as it describes the sharing in some common elements of life, if all good thoughts and holy desires do really proceed from God's Spirit, such a use of the word cannot be inaccurate or illegitimate; and it is most convenient to our purpose. Indeed it is very common for good and pious advisers of the faint-hearted to comfort them in their religious depression by assuring them that they are partakers of the divine nature to a much greater extent than they are aware. I then would merely push this possible dissidence between consciousness and reality to the extreme limit which facts require, and would maintain that God's creatures may be partakers of the divine nature without knowing it at all.

In this view it is evident that there is opened up to us an endless scale of degrees and disguises of which the attainment of creation's final cause is susceptible. Indeed the possibility of many degrees in attainment is suggested by St. Paul, when he hints that men may have to *feel after* God before they find Him. And surely they often feel after Him, when they know not at all what it is they want. Nay, in the sense which we have seen to be inherent in the word, there is some communion with God even in the humblest parts of creation. For there is a certain communion possible between the artist and his work, though indefinitely lower than that between a father and his children. A part of the worker himself has gone into his work: it appeals to him as it cannot do to any one else. A thing begotten, he knows not how, in the depths of his life beneath consciousness has risen more and more clearly into the surface light. And in his eager desire to give it the most articulate expression he has put it altogether outside him in the dry light of the outer world. But though it is outside him he feels as though his own life were in it; and in its reflection of his thought without the effort of conception, or at least in the communication and diffusion of the treasures hid in self, he finds perhaps some faint analogy to creative bliss. For so the Supreme Worker, we feel, must have a certain communion with landscape beauties, and organic wonders, with mountain heights and nestling violets, with leviathan in his strength, and with the lark in his ecstacy. I doubt not these are precious to the soul just because they are thoughts of God; they are great or beautiful because they are partakers of the divine nature. If we may dare to say it, they reflect God upon Himself: in them the treasures of his nature are diffused abroad; and He, the changeless, dwells in everlasting communion with the always changing universe, whose revolutions are phases of his glory. Thus no blossom drops, no withered leaf flitters down, but it enshrines its little part in the final cause of creation. For not at the birth of the world only, but now and for evermore the Divine Artist looks on all that his hands have made, "and behold it is very good."

But the Supreme Worker is a Father too; and in this relationship we believe Him to seek a higher communion, which bears a transcendental analogy to the most perfect communion of fathers and children on earth. The first approach to this higher communion was made, when the first moral sentiment was felt; and this relationship between God and Man will be consummated when all things are gathered into one in Christ, that is in the divine humanity. By a purely moral sentiment I mean the preference for an action because it is right, because it is kind or good, even at the expense of self, or at any rate apart from any consideration of comfort or convenience or advantage. If for example we may suppose that after ages of creative progress one of those dim flint-splitting creatures, who haunt the shadows on the borders of a past eternity, took pity on a wounded comrade left on an abandoned field and said 'I will carry him food and water though I die, for that is brave and right,' then I maintain that in him this higher divine communion was begun, though he could not know it as we do now. Only little by little would such moral sentiments acquire clear distinctness from the carnal life, and in the continuity of progress we can easily believe that the first steps might be imperceptible; but could they be traced, that would be the beginning of this higher communion with God, and an approximation towards the purest and intensest form of creation's final cause. But when men looked up to the glory of the dawn, and dreamed that day was poured from a source of light, supreme, unapproachable, which no man had seen or could see; when they began to associate that Shining One with the impartial sanction of the goodness they already loved, and to see in the lightning and the sun-stroke images of his vengeance against evil then the gates of a nearer access to the divine majesty were opened, and the possibility of a conscious communion with the Most High touched their hearts with a blessed awe.

I make no pretence at presenting anything but a possible outline of the earliest spiritual progress, an outline to which I shall ask attention again from another point of view.* The whole subject is yet far too obscure to allow any confident assertion of precise steps and their

---

* See Lecture II.

connection. But when I think how our faith in God and even the patent facts of spiritual consciousness are, by the perverse obstinacy of a zeal not according to knowledge, made to stand or fall with certain theories of human history which every year makes more untenable, I should be false to every highest duty of my vocation did I not attempt to show that the reality of our personal divine relationship is conceivably consistent with any scheme of the past that science can possibly propound. When I am summoned to stand and deliver on the one hand candour and common sense or on the other my faith in God, it is high time to show cause why I decline to do either.

It will easily be conceived that every movement in this high progress might be accompanied by eddying fancies or even back currents, by fetishism, or magic, or the wild theogonies of old; by devil-worship which passed backward through the beast to the demon; or by the material pantheism, which often, as in the case of Lucretius, had an inspiration little suspected by itself. But on the whole the history of human progress is the history of the growing purity and lustre with which this final cause of creation, creature life in God, has beamed forth on human souls. Prophets who heard in stillness and spoke in thunder, lawgivers who strove to bring down the marshalled order of the heavens on earth, poets who caught the subtle spirit of earthly beauty and breathed it from their lyres, psalmists who interpreted the meaning looks of sky and field and flood and found their whole significance to be the praise of God,—all had their part in attracting, in fixing the eye of conscience, and unfolding before it the splendour of its desire. To such as these, St. Peter says, "men did well that they gave heed, as unto a light shining in a dark place, until the day dawned, and the day-star arose in their hearts."\*

When the ideal of all purity, self-sacrifice and love stood on earth and said "he that hath seen me hath seen the Father," then the Day-star did arise in the hearts of men, bringing with it the dawn of a clearer and universal communion with God. That dawn, after what many think the darkest hour of night, appeared a sudden and startling brightness; but to us who are longing for high noon it may seem gradual and slow. Yet the divine consciousness of Christ has an exhaustless wealth of spiritual suggestion, which always re-animates our faith whenever we are brought into vital communion with him. And it is of this effect of his glorious personal life, not of the letter of the gospels, not of any dogmatic theology that I speak, when I say that at his coming suspicion changed to certainty and aspiration to a soul-felt grasp of God. Christ in his own manifest communion with the Father, and through the convictions he produced of the close and supernatural relation of God and man,—supernatural because transcending all phenomenal investigations—shed a light on

---

\* 2 Pet. i. 19. The apostle refers apparently to the second coming of Christ; but we may very well apply the words to a fuller apprehension of the Lord's spiritual work.

the dim desires of the soul, which brings the final cause of creation clearly into view, and awoke in human nature a spirit, which is nothing less than God's creative energy in the evolution of a better world. He awoke it by imparting not wisdom, not morality, not theology, but *himself* to mankind, by dying and entering into our life.* For "*the Lord is that Spirit,*" the spirit of the latter day, the spirit of truth, of candour, of reverence for fact, the spirit of high principle, self-sacrifice, divine communion. And they who are in that spirit, if still they seek the finger of God

> " in world or sun,
> In eagle's wing, or insect's eye,"

seek it not by way of proof that He is, but in communion with his creative joy, which they realize first of all by the sense of His work within their own souls. "The Lord is that Spirit;" and as the might of the sun is shown, not by the burning spot he makes in the blue of the sky, but by the wide atmosphere of light that

---

\* *How* Christ wrought this work for manhood, that is, what was the particular bearing thereon of his ministry, his suffering, his death and resurrection, is a question outside the limits of the present subject, and our ideas on that question are best formed gradually in the light of practical Christian experience. Teaching on such a subject may fairly be regarded as the main duty of the Christian ministry ; but it should be for the most part the teaching of the prophet "line upon line, precept upon precept, here a little and there a little." Thus is it best kept closely associated with a realization of the moral needs to which it applies : and without that association any attempt at systematic teaching on such a question too readily results in the substitution of opinion for faith, and of sectarian confidence for spiritual life.

fills, and by filling expands the world, so he who rightly uses the all pervasive spiritual light that streams from Christ better knows the power of the Sun of Righteousness, than he who too much concentrates his gaze on one dazzling spot in history. The healing, says the prophet, is in his wings, those wings of light that sweep the ever widening horizon of life.

Thus men have been feeling after God, that finding Him they might know the reason of their own being, and in it the final cause of creation. And though since the day of Christ, Christian opinion and organization have often undergone corruption and revolution, yet on the whole, whatever that narrow faith which is all but universal doubt may say, great progress has been made in that high quest; and, though some may scout it as a mere paradox, I verily believe that taking heart and intellect and moral life together man is nearer to God than ever. Our highly organized civilization is very probably more liable to some forms of evil, such as commercial conspiracies to defraud, and hopelessly demoralized pauperism, than were simpler states of society. And on the other hand we feel, more painfully than generations to whom the extent of the earth was little known, the vast expanse of barbarism. But on the whole public spirit never had higher aims; public opinion never was ruled by more purely ethical principles as distinguished from the passions of superstition; and the "enthusiasm of humanity," which is always kindled directly or indirectly by a sense of man's sacredness as

the son of God, was never more generally felt than at
the present day. Above all, science, politics, social life,
as well as spiritual revolutions, are working out at length
a true catholicity of religion, according to which the life
of God in the soul of man shall be freely reverenced
and loved, no matter what the intellectual form it may
take. At any rate the need of such a genuine catholicity
was never more widely realized. It presses itself upon
thousands of anxious hearts, who while they hold their
religious opinions dear, are galled to agony by the
limitations which such opinions *seem* to impose on the
recognition of earnestness, truth, and loyalty of soul
unless stamped as piety by some intellectual creed.
Meantime morbid developments of Christian dogma, and
the incongruous worldliness of Christian organizations
have led to many paradoxical reactions, in which the
very energy of faith in goodness drives men into the
forms of intellectual unbelief. What then? "*Is not
the life more than meat, and the body than raiment?*"
We cannot indeed pretend to the prerogative of God,
who alone looketh directly at the heart. But yet we
can discern through many an intellectual disguise the
emotional and moral life which is only possible by communion with God; and whether we can or can not
reconcile the evident fact with our opinions, we can at
least hold fast the fact, while the faith that is the living
soul of our opinions forces them to adapt themselves
to a wider catholicity of love. That seems at least
to be the lesson taught us and the example set by

the greatest and best amongst the leading spirits of the age.*

Yet let not any one think that this charity, which believeth all things and hopeth all things, can ever lessen our own joy in that faith which knows in whom it has believed. Our highest idea of manhood, and surely our truest conception of immortality, is still the contemplative but not necessarily inactive life, which, being consciously embraced by the love of God, finds in the universe an ever expanding revelation of his glory. And that life can be ours now only so far as we enter into the spirit of Christ.† "He that believeth on me," saith the Lord, "*hath* everlasting life;" and, making allowance for differences in forms of speech and thought, we cannot doubt that the essence of that belief is possession of the spirit of Christ. Most blessed are they who can apprehend in Christ a divinity beyond all other human experience, and who without fear of idolatry can worship God in him. "*Let us therefore as many as be perfect‡ be thus minded; and if in any respect*

---

\* That seems to me to have been especially the attitude suggested by Robertson, of Brighton, and A. J. Scott, of Manchester, of whom the former by his enormous posthumous influence, and the latter by a peculiar personal power of inspiration during his life, germinant in many minds since his death, have done more than many who in their lifetime bore greater names to strengthen religious faith during this sickly period of transition.

† This is surely the fundamental and universal sense of the words. "I am the way, the truth and the Life; no man cometh unto the Father but by me." John xiv. 6.

‡ The Greek τέλειοι does not necessarily involve the vain glorious assumption that seems to be in our English version. But to render

ye be otherwise minded, God shall reveal even this unto you. Nevertheless, whereto we have already attained, let us walk by the same rule, let us mind the same thing." If we are lowly reverent, aspiring and devoted, this is the real spirit of Christ; and in it we shall experience the truth of the prophetic testimony, "*to this man will I look, even to him that is poor, and of a contrite spirit, and trembleth at my word.*" "*The secret of the Lord is with them that fear him.*" Surely in words of inspiration like these there is an endless germinative power to fill with spiritual life the widest horizon of knowledge. For what is the secret of the Lord but this, that all life is a communion with the Heavenly Father, all beauty a glimpse of His light, all joy a share in His bliss, all struggle and sorrow but a hint of the ineffable burden that He bears "in bringing many sons unto glory?" He then who has this blessed secret knows why he lives, and why creation enspheres his life, and why the whole world groans and travails in pain together until now. Such an experience when bright and clear is heaven begun on earth; it is a draught from that "river of God's pleasures," which some day we shall follow up to its source behind the veil. And he with whom is this secret of the Lord can look, if with painful longing, yet without despair on all the darkness of the world's mystery of sin. For his own experience tells him that

---

"completely initiated." which I believe St. Paul to have meant, would seem harsh and pedantic.

God is not very far from every one of us. His own communion with God he values, not as a personal or sectarian peculiarity, but as a token of the divine kinship of all mankind. Indeed herein often lies the distinction between genuine religious experience and mere sectarian fanaticism. For the one makes us more human than before, brings us down from our personal isolation unto the deeper region of life, which, though beneath the surface of consciousness in many, is nevertheless we feel a generic attribute of man. The other shuts us up in self or sect, and makes us feel as the detestable Calvinistic sentiment has it—

"a garden walled around,
Chosen and made peculiar ground."

Nor is this all the distinction. Sectarian fanaticism will generally be found to eye the future with gloomy fear, sweetened only by the fierce joy of personal salvation as a brand snatched from a burning world. But he who feels most profoundly God's essential nearness to himself, will derive from that a secure and sometimes triumphant confidence that one day God will be all in all. The present life we have in God should rid us from any slavish dependence on the letter of Scripture. Therefore we shall not try to guess the future of earth and heaven from peddling criticism of words, which, however divine in spiritual suggestion, were specially adapted to times when the only available forms of speech and thought were inseparable from utter misconceptions of the universe. The dawning of God's presence in ourselves, interpreted by the general continuity of progress, is the most certain prophecy we can have of the final and universal prevalence of life in Him. The feeling that the final cause of our own creation is our joy in God and his joy in us assures us that the mystery of God can never be finished until the kingdoms of heaven and earth and hell are delivered up to the Father, that He may be all in all.

# LECTURE II.

---

## THE GOD-CONSCIOUSNESS IN HUMANITY.

"*Nevertheless I am continually with thee.*"—Ps. lxiii. 23.

"*If haply they might feel after Him, and find Him though He be not far from every one of us.*"—Acts xvii. 27.

THE phrase, 'God-consciousness,' awkwardly imitated from the German, sounds no doubt harshly to English ears, and it is as well to confess at once that I am about to give to it a wider sense than perhaps is usual. But whether I could have used any better words to express my meaning I must leave you to judge after that meaning is unfolded. I will only by way of anticipation say that it at least expresses a present actual fact of human life. And this much at least we owe to the "Positive Philosophy," that we are driven more than ever to seek the roots of religious conviction as well as of scientific knowledge in the undeniable realities of experience. Besides, I have said 'in humanity' rather than 'in man,' because I do not mean an occasional or even the great phenomenon of experience, but a constituent element in human nature, a faculty so irrepressible and universal, that if it be blocked in one direction it almost invariably re-appears in another; an instinct so deep that even where it does not appear in the articulate consciousness of the individual, it broods in an impersonal form round the bases of the life of his race. For every single member of a tribe or nation may be wholly without any perception of personal communion with a living eternal Spirit, while yet in the ideal aspirations, or, if you will, in the superstitious habits which move or control the community there may be significant indications of that element in humanity which is the subject of our thoughts.

If I read aright the signs of the times, the interpretation to be given to this element in human nature is likely to become more and more the one religious question; and will perhaps be felt to carry within itself the decision of all others worth contending about. And farther one may venture to say that if only earnest appreciative attention can be secured to the thing itself, the mere name that shall be given to it is at most a secondary question, and by no means so vital as some appear to think. For men otherwise lost in doubt, may still be candid, still be faithful to what they feel to be the noblest instincts of their nature. And if so, I maintain they may be practically obeying the God-consciousness within them, even though through intellectual error they may call it by another name. Let a man realize with awe the vastness of creation and the depth of life; let him realize the supersensuous significance of the perceptions of conscience, and own the power of its imperial voice; let him measure self against the universe, and feel that while his place is that of a sacrifice to higher ends yet in the conscious act of sacrifice he is greater than all the material world—why then we must at least own that he is loyal to his high vocation as a man. But if he should say 'I know, I feel all this, yet what you call God I call, alas! I know not what,—shall we then cry Anathema! atheist! fool? Nay rather, surely Maranatha! the Lord is at hand,—thou art not far from the kingdom of God.

I am too well aware of the anxieties felt by many minds at the present time to doubt for a moment that the words already uttered may suggest or rewaken more questions than we can hope to solve. But the most important of such questions I think I can catch, though the lips of the questioners are silent. 'Tell us more plainly what you mean,' says one; 'have we all this God-consciousness, as you call it, whether we believe in God or not?' 'Of what use then is the Bible,' asks another; 'or what is the relation of this faculty to revelation?' 'Nay rather,' asks a third, 'how can the existence of such an element in man be harmonized with the theories of man's physical origin which scientific men begin to regard as already proved?' 'After all,' says a fourth more practical, 'what is it worth, this God-consciousness in man?

Can it give us the strength to live or die?' To such questions as these I hope to give at least some hint of answer; and to deal with some of them more fully in the following lectures. Meanwhile I will endeavour first to explain more clearly the meaning I associate with this phrase, the 'God-consciousness in humanity.' Then afterwards I will venture to offer certain suggestions as to the probable history of this faculty. And without endorsing any scientific theories yet in dispute, I trust these suggestions may be found consistent with any possible theory about the physical origin of man. Finally, I should like to say something on the practical bearings of the question, that is on the moral and spiritual value of the God-consciousness in humanity.

I.

Although the phrase which describes our subject is undeniably an awkward one, yet after all it carries its meaning on its front. It expresses a mingling of God with our personal life. It is in fact a short and emphatic way of putting St. Paul's words "*in Him we live, and move, and have our being.*" No doubt the phrase in its German original means properly a consciousness of God. But I prefer the other and more awkward rendering, because it is more open to the wider meaning which I am desirous of associating with it. 'Consciousness of God' would express both more and less than I wish to convey—intensively more, extensively less. I do not say that every man is directly conscious of such ideas as may be suggested to our minds by the name of God, or by the phrase communion with God. The position I take is this. I find certain elements in my own deepest life, elements which experience, nay, which my *generic* consciousness itself assures me are common to all mankind, and which when closely examined seem to me necessarily to involve God and my moral relationship to Him. I may of course be pointed to individual men here and there to whom these elements however closely examined do *not* seem to involve God. But then I do not feel driven to seek uncharitable reasons for this. Be it so, I would say, yet these men have what we call the God-consciousness nevertheless; and if I can induce them to give more heed to these divine elements in consciousness, even though they may never in this life put the same interpretation upon them that I do, I shall not have spoken in vain.

Before we go any farther it may be necessary to say a few words in explanation of a perhaps unusual phrase which I have just used, and which has I venture to think an important bearing upon our present enquiry. I refer to the term *generic* as distinguished from *individual* consciousness. By this I mean the consciousness which we instinctively take for granted that we share with the whole of our race, as contrasted with what we feel to be personal peculiarities of ourselves or of a limited number. However the propriety of the term may be disputed, some such distinction certainly exists; whether wholly the growth of experience or not, I shall not care to dispute. There are certainly some things which you readily believe to be characteristic only of yourselves and a few more. There are others which you cannot help feeling confident you share with the whole race. For example, there may be some one amongst you with such a genius for calculation, that the moment a complicated arithmetical problem is put before him, he has what seems an instinctive perception of the result. This he will know of course to be peculiar to himself. But if you were to tell him of a race of men who could not distinguish between one and two, or two and three, and who never thought of counting their cows, or pigs or canoes, he would probably reply, you are not telling me of men but of monkeys; I will believe in no such race; for the tendency to numeration is an essential element in humanity. Such a man would be speaking out of his generic consciousness; and if I say that he would be perfectly right, I do not mean that he would be justified in denying that there ever were anthropomorphous creatures who could not count; but only that such a deficiency would put them outside of the properly human kind. Man, however he came to be constituted as at present, has certainly a notion of a generic inner nature, as well as a power of recognizing the generic outward form; and a race of creatures who could not count three would no more be men than a race of creatures with hairy bodies and prehensile feet and tails. Similarly, a man who is conscious of such delight in the pursuit of truth that he prefers abstract speculation to money-making, knows well enough that in this respect he is in a minority. But if he were told of a tribe who could watch a thunderstorm or an eclipse without a trace of wonder or imaginative awe, he would probably be incredulous; at least his generic consciousness would suggest that such a form of human nature was in the highest degree unlikely. Still farther if he were told of beings in the shape of men who cared nothing at all about the reason why; who could see a watch or a mechanical toy for the first time, and neither form nor try to form any theory whatever about the cause of its movements, his generic consciousness would urge him to suspect unfairness in the account, or if not, to insist that whether through imperfect development, or because of degradation, such creatures were below the level of humanity. These observations will show that the idea of a generic consciousness is not to be taken in too extended a significance. Assuming for a moment, what many of high authority hold to be most probable, that man has gradually risen through lower grades to be what he is now, then this generic consciousness may include many pre-historic races, but by no means necessarily all. By humanity we mean

"Men our brothers, men the workers, ever learning something new."

—not any creature hovering between ape and man. I confess I do not fear the alarming inferences which some suppose to be involved in the gradual instead of sudden creation of mankind. However it came to be, this generic consciousness for which I contend is now an actual fact. And it associates with the idea of humanity a spiritual nature, which remains the same whatever may have been the means which God has used for calling it forth. Nay we may conceive that should this theory be ultimately established, it may even relieve us of the pressure of some difficulties. For as our generic consciousness does not feel bound to gather all possible pre-historic races into its embrace, so its confidence need not necessarily be shaken by isolated instances of apparent exception at the present day. If for instance a Bushman, or an Andaman Islander, or an Australian Savage be—though I do not acknowledge that these races are—in any respect outside its range, all we can say is that such races must have stopped short of, or fallen below the generic inner idea of humanity. It is as an essential element in this generic inner idea of humanity that I am anxious to look at the God-consciousness now.

In the book of Job, Elihu, in the heat of a vehement re-action against what he thinks the ignoble tone of the other speakers, exclaims "*but there is a spirit in man, and the inspiration of the Almighty hath given them understanding.*" This is plainly an utterance of his generic consciousness. And we all know moments of sacred passion when our souls hear ringing in his words the key-note of the highest human life. Now what does such an utterance mean to us when it affects us so?

Surely we do not interpret it then as a philosophical or metaphysical proposition about the relations of body and soul. We love it rather because it gives articulate expression to an experience which is very dear to us. "There is a spirit in man" means simply then, there is something in us deeper than self or sense. And the "inspiration of the Almighty" expresses our feeling of direct dependence for this inner life on "that which made the world so fair." "There is a spirit in man:" we are not wholly the slaves of pleasures and of pains, of mercenary gain or loss; there is a keen unutterable joy in the pursuit of truth for its own sake, in self-sacrificing love, in longing contemplations of the mystery of life. In such moments the God-consciousness speaks out. It is the deep and fiery energy of a divine impulse breaking through the cold hard surface of our self-containment; it is our oneness with the substance of the world re-acting against the superficial intensity of our individual isolation. When, in a time of perplexity and temptation, you say 'I will do the right thing, then let come on what may,' what is the secret of the strange stern joy you feel? When, in painful doubt, you say to timid teachers 'don't talk of safety and prudence, tell us only the truth,' what is the inspiration of your strong desire? When you have for once, in secret and unpraised, made an unreserved sacrifice of yourself for a cause that touched your hearts, what was the balm that dropped into your soul, and made a holier peace than you had ever known? I am persuaded that were it not incongruous even to think of self-scrutiny in such exalted moments, you would feel that the secret of this spiritual glory was a sense of oneness with an order grander than material laws, with an all-pervading life in which for ever all is well, with an all-embracing love, to be at one with which is your heart's final joy.

I know very well the claims or hopes of physiological research to show for every spiritual emotion a vibration in the brain. I know how laws of association with lower pleasures are invoked to account for strains of thought which seem rather an echo of the harps of heaven. Nor can I, like a jealous landed proprietor, build out by walls of prejudice obtrusive fact, then take my pleasure in my narrow garden as though such things were not. I am content with a conviction which is as impregnable as a mathematical axiom, that however accurately or exhaustively science may display the accompanying conditions, or material phenomena of thought, it never can produce a feeling of conscious identity with nerve vibrations; it never can effect such a realization to self of an existence terminable inwards by the anatomy of the brain, as would alone avail to disturb the God-consciousness in man. After all, brain is only a phenomenon, or collection of phenomena; and however completely a correspondence could be shown between its variations and variations of another kind in the phenomena of consciousness, the two things compared are to every sense or perception we possess so entirely different, that their ultimate unity must be conceived as concealed in the true substance underlying them both. Now physical science does not affect to deal with substance. But so far as its subtle analysis, its revelations of infinity in an atom, its generalizations concerning force give any hint, it is certainly adverse to the gross materialism which really identifies *material phenomena* with substance. If the epithet 'material' means anything, it ought to signify everything that appeals to the bodily senses. And if that be so science knows nothing material except forms of force, or if you will, forces. That is, it follows up all material phenomena to a kind of border land, beyond which it loses them in a certainly *immaterial* mystery. No one then under any conceivable condition of science could be entitled to say 'brain tissue is the substance of which our consciousness is the mere phenomenon.' It will always be open to reply that we recognise brain energy as a form of force, *so far as observation goes* inextricably associated with the definite forms assumed by consciousness. All the admission amounts to is this, that brain seems to be a condition necessary to the limitation or definition of that portion of universal substance which takes form in human personal life; but whether that condition be initial and temporary, or permanent and essential, there is on this mode of enquiry no evidence to show. But to suppose that science tends to prove brain only substantial and mind an 'eidolon,' is a delusion which it would be most unjust to charge on the greatest and most uncompromising physicists of the day. They know nothing of substance and care to know nothing, save only in some moments of wistful reverie when "what they seem" would so fain "behold what is, and no man understands." And in such moments I maintain that men are nearer to the substance of the universe than in any scientific generalization. It is the God-consciousness that enthrones us above a visionary world.

I believe that this divine element in us appears sometimes as pure reason, sometimes as spiritual imagination, sometimes as conscience, thus presenting a triune manifestation of the one God-consciousness in man. I need not stop to discuss the question of pure reason as between one school of philosophy and another. Even granting that every universal judgment which we form, and every supersensuous aspiration which we breathe is the issue of experience, still experience requires two factors, the subject and the object; and the forms which experience takes in consciousness must owe something to each of these. Let it be granted for instance that the universal judgment, "things which are equal to the same are equal to one another," is not merely suggested but learned by experience. Still, the fact that experience takes this form is due to a certain susceptibility in the nature which is educated up to that point by experience. And this susceptibility has a right to consideration just as much as the phenomena which influence and educate it. For the purpose of our present argument then, I am content that the pure reason should take the lowest form that can well be assigned to it. For if there is in our personal life a susceptibility which under impressions from the external world is led inevitably and universally to certain judgments which we cannot conceivably reverse, we should be disloyal to the order of the universe if we did not hold that these judgments involved an ultimate truth. I hold then that there are some deeply-seated convictions or impressions—call them intuitions, call them conclusions or what you will,—such as no science which deals with appearances can possibly overthrow. Pure reason insists that appearances or phenomena always imply substance; it suggests that ultimately all substance is one, and thus sets us groping towards God. Pure reason insists on cause, and so step by step leads us back towards God. It joins cause to force, and force to living will, and so draws us up to God. So long as men keep within the limits of the practical understanding which is content with calculating the chances of phenomenal succession and acting accordingly, there is nothing to open the inward vista which looks to the infinite. But no sooner do we realize the impulse to distinguish what *seems* from what *is*, what moves from what is moved, than a door is opened in heaven, and we hear a voice saying, "come up hither."

Yet we do not in fact ascend thither unless reason is winged by spiritual imagination. By this phrase I mean of course not the more or less sensuous faculty which builds out of the ruins of memory an ideal outward world, but rather the same energy of the soul, which engenders the longing after a final cause, the contemplative gaze which dotes upon the vision of life, until its depths open up and its inward meaning dawns. The spiritual imagination, aroused by perceptions of congruity and beauty as real and far more searching than the sight of the eyes, roams through the universe seeking some object of supreme adoration,— an object apart from which, existence seems not an enigma only, but a contradiction to every demand of reason, to every longing of the heart and every conviction of the conscience. The spiritual imagination may be poetic, mystic, vague, even visionary, but it is no liar; and its unconquerable feeling that the life of humanity cannot be alone in the universe commends itself after all to the most dispassionate judgment.

Of the conscience we have in effect already spoken. I only desire now to add that in its sense of a supreme eternal authority as the ultimate sanction of right it is the most commonly realized aspect of the God-consciousness in man. Whatever theory is held of the moral standard, whether it is supposed to make its appeal to a special intuitive perception, or is regarded as the product of utilitarian experience and transferred associations, the sanction which binds us to obey is a wholly distinct question; and no satisfactory account can be given of this, which does not in one form or another involve, what we may call the common sense view, 'I must, I ought, because God wills it.' Say that a man is bound to live in harmony with the order of the universe, say that he is bound to contribute his part to the common good. I do not deny that he may feel the force of this without ever asking the reason why. But it is not the less true that in this feeling the righteous and loving Life which embraces all things manifests itself in him though he may not know it. And in this obscure inarticulate sense of indefeasible obligation I recognize the God-consciousness of humanity.

Once more I repeat that the possession of this divine sense does not necessarily bring any man consciously into personal communion with God. But it does tend to this: it does come very near to it. "*I girded thee though thou hast not known me*" is a prophetic word applicable to more than Cyrus, and in a deeper sense than the prophet's immediate meaning. Many a man, who in early life has given little attention to religious thought, feels in after times of deep spiritual experience that God has been with him and in him all his days. While therefore I cannot maintain that the God-consciousness always involves a realization of communion with a living Person, I contend that it does bear out the words of St. Paul, "He is not far from every one of us;" it does lead up to God; it does give everlasting meaning to the revelation in Jesus Christ; and when realised as belonging to the generic consciousness of mankind, it does give an undying interest and significance to all religious history. Of one thing at least we may be confident: it will for ever forbid Atheism as the finality of human thought. As the soul's longing for a final cause still utters its sigh when apparently crushed out by the dead weight of materialism, so the God-consciousness in general even where to the intellect there is no God, wakes afresh in cravings for religion such as followed the completion of the Positive Philosophy. Nor was Comte so inconsistent as many suppose, however melancholy the fantastic development of his positive religion may have been. For if Positivism means taking facts as they stand, it was impossible in the science of humanity to ignore the feelings and affections which generate religion. An essential condition of our highest life is some supreme loyalty, for which Humanity has been offered as the object, but which that is neither spiritually definite nor morally exalted enough to command. It lacks the majesty of eternity; it has no tenderness like the name of Our Father; it is too evidently a laboured abstraction to excite the passion of worship. But if a man should say I worship the universe,—the All in All,—I should be bold to say, sir, you worship God, though you call Him by another name, and approach Him from another aspect. For a man cannot worship a *thing* however big; and the moment he talks of a harmony order and beauty that touch his heart, he shows a sense of a hidden life, which I welcome as a sign that the God-consciousness is awake within him. Should mankind then be driven in a momentary maze into intellectual atheism, what would they do with this obstinate irrepressible faculty, the religious nature, which we sum up as the God-consciousness? Its beginning and end would be theoretically cut off, its origin and inspiration gone, but still it would not, could not die. I have seen a so-called air-plant clinging to a little bit of wood suspended by a string. But even this has fibres which grasp the wood, and pores which drink in the moisture and gases of the air. And no freak of nature, no miracle indeed, unless the creation of something out of nothing, could rival the harsh discontinuity with the reality of things which would be presented by a God-consciousness without a God. It would be a universal aspiration without an aim, a restless mystic tendency without any conceivable adequate impulse, a lie inherent in the generic consciousness of man, a fundamental discord in the highest results of creation. Surely mute inanimate law, which necessarily carries within itself only the germs of action congruous with itself, could never produce so cruel an issue as this. Such a law would keep all things within the symmetry of nature, and not a thought of man could have wandered beyond. Under such a law there could have been no dream of God to burn its creatures with vain desire, and make the *truth* abhorrent to their noblest affections. No: if living love is not creation's final law, there is something in the constitution of the universe which looks like malice. The God-consciousness in humanity inevitably involves either religion or superstition: the world is ruled either by God or Devil: and no one who feels *that* issue will hesitate about his choice.

## II.

The question then naturally arises, what is the relation of all this to the Bible and the Christian revelation? "You tell us," it may be said, "of a voice in every man throughout the race speaking of God; what then was the use of the voices of Sinai, or of the utterances of prophets and apostles? We read in the Scriptures that man fell from a state of happy innocence and utterly died to God. Did he not at the same time lose his God-consciousness and all heavenly inspiration unless by special grace?" Others again from a different point of view may ask, "supposing the theory of the natural origin as distinguished from the instantaneous creation of man to be established, as some who are best able to judge think it will be, if it is not established already, how will your opinions consist with this?" I shall give my answer to both sets of enquiries in the form of a hint—I can scarcely call it a sketch—of the probable history of the God-consciousness in man. We have already seen the fundamental impossibility that scientific investigations of material phenomena can affect the substantial nature of present spiritual facts. But discoveries as to the history of the material world do affect the *process* by which those spiritual facts have come to be what they are. Whether God made man out of an anthropomorphous ape, or made him directly out of inorganic dust, either way He made him a man; and the decision of the question cannot alter the meaning of the word; but it must necessarily alter our opinions about the history of the spiritual consciousness which is an essential element in that meaning. And here I take leave to protest against the senseless use which is sometimes made of the solemn truism—'religion is one thing, science another.' If it be meant that they approach the central Truth from different sides, and that the one mode of access leads more deeply into the heart of it than the other; or in other words, if it be meant that science deals with phenomena of one kind, and religion with phenomena of another, but phenomena much more significantly suggestive of ultimate substance, that is all very well. But when as is sometimes the case this formula is used to justify the holding of two directly contrary sets of opinions on the same subjects, one can hardly refrain from characterizing it as a subterfuge of spiritual cowardice. It is perfectly consistent to say 'my heart holds to the living God as the substance of all things, a faith no scientific theory can touch.' But it is not consistent, and but for the effect of custom would be felt to be sheer self-stultification for an accomplished geologist solemnly to declare as a fact that " *God spake all these words, saying, . . . in six days the LORD made heaven and earth, the sea and all that in them is, and rested the seventh day.*" In regard to many religious opinions it is not true that religion is one thing and science another. They represent simply opposite judgments on the same facts in the same aspect of them, that is, their historical reality; and therefore one or the other must be false. Of course scientific theories are often formed very rashly and are often superseded. But that *some* theories totally inconsistent with old religious opinions are finally established, only stolidity, or a faith desperate through ignorance of its own immortal essence, can possibly deny. And surely it is intolerable to go on any longer holding our religious faith as though on sufferance of imperfect knowledge,—miserable to hold our ground like tenants along the line of an unfinished railway, who hope against hope that bankruptcy of the company or some diversion may occur to save their old habitations. It is necessary not merely to yield a grudging admission to such new facts as are thrust upon our attention, but also if possible once for all to take some view of the spiritual nature which shall be entirely independent of all contingencies of future opinion, because it can afford scope for them all. I have tried to keep this object before me in the remarks made hitherto; and at this point I am particularly anxious it should be understood that I do not undertake—it is no part of my duty—to recommend this or that scientific speculation which may yet be in dispute, but to show that the view of the God-consciousness which I have urged gives ample room for all.

In attempting to give any hint as to the probable history of the God-consciousness in humanity, we grant at once that the Bible does not yield us the means of observing its earliest manifestations. For whatever fragmentary reminiscences of prehistoric Hebrew origins scholars may think they can disinter from the early chapters of Genesis, it is useless in the present state of archæological research to contend for the historical character of the narrative in which they are imbedded. Such reminiscences have their value; but as for the primeval beginnings of human history, they leave these in utter impenetrable darkness. On the other hand, the farther prehistoric archæology advances, the more remote does the first appearance of man upon the earth appear to be; while at the same time indications multiply which suggest that only by slow degrees did he assume mentally and spiritually the full proportions of humanity. As to the mode of his creation we have no need here to decide. It is sufficient if we exhibit a theory of his spiritual nature consistent with acknowledged facts, and dependent on no contingencies of any controversy that may yet be undecided.\* We only assume that the history is an inconceivably long one, and that its first indications suggesting a very low condition appear to many to imply a previous progress from a condition lower still. But God's purposes concerning mankind were from the very beginning marked in the bodily form he gave them—a form which by whatever process it was originated was equally the work of God—a form which in itself was a prophecy that a spiritual kingdom of God was at hand. The signs of mental supremacy

\* Note B on the relation of the Development Theory to Immortality.

over the world would soon be manifest. Little by little, we may suppose, the mind of man rose to a self-consciousness clearly separable from merely animal instincts. And when once he could so far stand distinct from and over against nature as to feel wonder, the life of contemplation was begun, and at least the germ of the God-consciousness was formed. For the sense of wonder involves the realization of a disturbed unity which the soul struggles to restore. And here we have the beginning both of science and religion, which like highly differentiated organs in the mature animal, may very well have been indistinguishable in their germs. The sense of wonder too is closely akin to that of awe, and easily suggests some Unknown Power which from the vast beyond breaks through the limits of vision and manifests itself in the marvellous object of contemplation. But it is the distinct consciousness, involved in wonder, of self as separate from and set over against Nature, on which I would most insist. This would suggest the possibility of overcoming natural forces by skill, as for instance of conquering the wolf by the stone hatchet, or the elephant by the pitfall; while, on the other hand, it would beget a tenderer feeling towards human kind, exhibited first of all towards members of the same horde or clan, but leading on towards the recognition of a mystic sacredness in man. In all this there was assuredly the teaching of God, "the inspiration of the Almighty," although a spiritual conception, nay the very notion of His being might yet be unformed.

But the sharper grew the contrast between Man and Nature, the more would wonder and reflection be awakened by the sunset and the dawn, by the woodland vista and the deep abyss, above all, perhaps, by the thunderstorm, the earthquake or the eclipse. Thus, it may be, was engendered the first tendency to worship. For if it is true that the highest civilization is the result of long fermentation amongst inferior elements often utterly unlike itself, there can be little difficulty in recognizing, what many phenomena among barbarous religions would suggest, that the noblest sentiments of love and reverence for an Almighty Father are connected in a direct line of ascent with the dread felt by the savage of the Power that can withhold the sunlight or shake the solid ground. Probably the first signs of conscience would be shown in loyalty to the interests of the village or the tribe. But as the sense of an Unseen Power grew more and more upon the soul, an association would be gradually realized between the voice of conscience and the authority of the gods. Then as wonder at the greatness of nature deepened into reverence and awe, breaking sometimes into love, and sometimes into dread, the heart would long for some word from the unseen; and if we say that the spiritual imagination supplied this want, let it not be supposed for a moment that this implies the unreality of all divine communications with the soul of man. On the contrary, according to the view taken now, that craving for a word from the unseen was itself a divine suggestion, and the meeting of that want through the avenue of the spiritual imagination was just a mingling of divine inspirations and human thoughts, capable of all modifications of degree up to the visions of an Isaiah or a Paul.

The danger of misconception here arises from the strange but inveterate tendency to suppose that divine action is necessarily sudden, complete, and incapable of progress through various degrees of perfection. When geology first became a science many seemed to think that it necessarily ignored, or rather denied the agency of a Creator. For if God did not make the universe in six days, and each main division of it in a second of time, they could not conceive that God made it at all. So when it began to be maintained that species are the result of gradually accumulating modifications of structure, inherited by successive generations, many seemed to impersonate Development as a sort of huge ugly idol which was set up as a rival to the Creator. They could not conceive that it was really God who made an elephant, unless he did it in one particular way, that is, unless he gathered a heap of inorganic dust together and commanded it instantly to become a living animal. If the theory of the *process* be changed, and instead of springing instantly out of inorganic dust, the elephant is supposed to be the result of successive modifications according to an ascertainable law, then to such minds as these it seems that divine energy is entirely eliminated from the process, and creation explained without God. Yet a little reflection would show that it is just as easy to conceive of God working gradually as suddenly; and a little more reflection would show that no theory which touches the process implies any opinion one way or the other as to the original energy by which the process is worked out.*

So with regard to the growth of the God-consciousness in man; let no one think for a moment that if we believe its origin, like all other origins, to be lost in mystery, and its progress to have been gradual, that we therefore empty it of inspiration. Not one step in the whole process can be rationally accounted for apart from the inspiration of the Almighty, least of all the deep instinctive association of conscience with the voice of God. But I am assuming that inspiration all through, and only pointing out the steps by which it may be conceived as advancing.

There is nothing unnatural or arbitrary in the supposition that the God-consciousness might be developed much more rapidly in some races than in others. The extent to which it did so is not a matter of faith, but simply of historical enquiry. But there can hardly be any dispute that amongst the Jews its pre-eminence became the distinguishing characteristic of their national life. And accordingly to deny an unusual degree of inspiration in their case would be as absurd as to suppose that the God-consciousness was awakened in man without any inspiration at all. Farther, that

* See Appendix, Note C.

extraordinary inspiration may affect the ordinary relations between human volition and surrounding phenomena is an idea not necessarily opposed, so far as I am aware, to any *established* conclusions in philosophy or science. Believing as I do that the only ultimate force is the energy of God, and that this is the energy of a free and loving Will, I have no sympathy with any tendency to impose the limit of experience on possibility, or to say that no evidence can prove a miracle. That such a thing is on merely natural grounds, that is, from observations on the regularity of nature, highly improbable, I fully admit; that it requires uncommonly strong evidence to prove it I allow; and I conjecture farther that even where proved, it would be found, if we could know all about it, to be simply the supersession of a lower order by a higher. The issue is that the reality or non-reality of miraculous occurrences is not necessarily a matter of religious faith: but that it *is* necessarily a question of historical evidence in which testimony should be scrutinized with unusual care; while the moral and spiritual interests of mankind, and the Godward direction of the highest progress should have due weight in determining the degree of possibility or probability that some such extraordinary manifestations of power might mark great eras in universal history. Looking in such a frame of mind at the narratives which describe the growth of the God-consciousness amongst the Jews, we should be disposed to say that as regards the Old Testament we have really no historical evidence to go upon, at least none sufficient to maintain by its own force the stupendous and sometimes apparently gratuitous miracles it enshrines. And therefore the amount of belief which men accord to those miracles will be found to depend simply on the extent to which they think them to have been necessary for the religious education of mankind. For myself I do not believe that the literal truth of Old Testament miracles can be maintained on this ground alone. The history is most suggestive and impressive. It shows many tokens of a special inspiration in the Israelitish race and its writers. Its preservation is a rich blessing to the world; yet that blessing consists not in any literally accurate preservation of the external history of the Jews, but much more in the helps it gives to the imagination in realizing the impulses of their inner life. That God revealed Himself in visions, I do not at all doubt; but in producing them the Divine Spirit wrought through the nerves and brain of the excited seer. That miracles may have been wrought in those early days I have no wish to deny: but the evidence for individual instances has not come down to us in a form which will bear historical criticism. All that remains and must always remain perfectly certain is this, that the Jewish race became the natural and inevitable line of the highest development of the God-consciousness in man, which in this pre-eminent line reached in Christ a critical culmination such as introduced a wholly new era, and almost a new species of man.

On reaching the ministry of Christ I contend that we enter at once into the light of historical evidence. I do not indeed suppose for a moment that the Gospel narratives are perfectly and uniformly accurate. But the variety and congruity of the evidence connecting them with the living testimony of Apostles are to my mind so resistless, and the idea of falsehood on their part is to me so impossible, that as a matter of historical opinion I am compelled to regard the narrative, miracles included, as substantially true. On the other hand it seems not unworthy of the Most High that the stupendous energy of a spiritual life, which so dominated the future of the world, should be associated with a command of nature such as set before the wondering eyes of simple men the most expressive symbols of saving grace. At the same time a judgment on historical evidence cannot be regarded as a matter of religious faith. I know it may be urged that spiritual sympathies necescessarily affect our judgment of evidence; but if it is meant that the historical evidence for Christian miracles leaves no room for difference of opinion except what is occasioned by varieties of spiritual sympathy, candour as to my own feeling compels me to demur. Still farther, if it is meant that historical disbelief of the Christian miracles necessarily implies an unchristian heart, there are facts to the contrary so patent and undeniable, that he who can ignore them would, if born a Jew at the Christian era, have refused to believe the resurrection of Christ though he had seen it with his own eyes.

To me, while I hold fast to the historical facts, these are but the "flesh and blood" to which our Heavenly Father has "linked a truth divine." The appearance of Jesus on the field of history may be regarded as a crisis of universal progress greater than the birth into the world of the first creature that could be called a man. So far St. Paul's parallel and contrast between Adam and Christ would be tenable on any theory. For a new race was born in Christ; the divine humanity to which God is not Object only but Subject.\* Up to Christ's day the God-consciousness had availed mainly to give significance to the tokens of God's being which were more objectively than subjectively regarded, whether seen in vision or in outward events. But the one preeminently distinctive characteristic of the Lord Jesus is his intense, marvellous, unwavering consciousness of God. In the sunny clearness of the synoptic discourses which like a summer day hide their depth in light, in the dimmer vistas opened up into the mind of the Lord by the discourses of the fourth gospel, in such words as "the Father that dwelleth in me, He doeth the works," and even in the apparently despairing cry, "My God, my God why hast thou forsaken me," we

\* For this suggestion I am indebted to the remark of a friend who probably would not desire to have his name mentioned in these pages.

have the manifestations of a life of which God was felt to be the inmost substance as well as the basis and the law and the glory of creation. I have little sympathy with the efforts that are sometimes made to describe the nature of the Incarnation in pseudo-ontological essays. It is sufficient for me to recognize and to worship a fulness of divinity in Christ which makes him the most perfect expression to us of what God is in moral relations, and of what man may be in communion with God. Henceforward, without any dislocation or break of continuity in the spiritual history of the race, men were to learn that in seeking after God they need not ascend into the heavens nor descend into the abyss, because the word is nigh them in their hearts. Henceforward men were to grow in the knowledge of God, not merely as the supreme *Object* of contemplation reflected from all the works of nature, but also as the inmost *Subject* deeper than self-consciousness, but coming to light in ever-recurrent inspirations. In this point of view we may mark a special significance in the mission of the Comforter, so prominent a feature of the Christian dispensation. With this tendency of Christ's religion also we may connect the promise of the Lord, "*if a man love me he will keep my words, and my Father will love him, and we will come unto him and take up our abode with him.*" Surely this implies that the spiritual consciousness of Christ was to be renewed in his people according to their measure. In this direction we may look for the fulfilment of some of the most mysterious longings and promises of the Lord. "*The glory which thou gavest me I have given them; that they may be one even as we are one; I in them and thou in me, that they may be made perfect in one,—and I have declared unto them thy name, and will declare it, that the love wherewith thou hast loved me may be in them and I in them.*" Strange as these words may sound to some, they have a very practical significance to those who can feel with St. Paul, that God "has revealed his Son in them." "*For God who commanded the light to shine out of darkness hath shined in our hearts, to give the light of the knowledge of the glory of God in the face of Jesus Christ.*" So every man who knows God in Christ may enjoy a God-consciousness, the calm intensity and filial confidence of which surpass all prophetic vision. And I maintain that the real matter of interest for us is practically to enter into that diviner manhood which feels God to be the soul of its soul as well as the substance of the world. Theoretic questions as to the precise nature of Christ's person will perhaps never be set at rest, unless by the prevalence of a deeper philosophy of the relations of man to God and of the creature to the Creator. If I feel that I am brought nearer to God through Christ, if I realize through faith in him as a true manifestation of God a keenness of self-reproach, a glow of love, a self-sacrificing zeal that intensifies every best element in my nature; whatever theory I may hold concerning his person, or even if I have no theory at all, he is to me the power of God unto salvation.

We need not follow the history of the God-consciousness beyond the appearance of Christ. Indeed all the latter-day glory of which we make our boast, even those triumphs of science which some foolishly suppose to be at the expense of religion, are only a fuller expansion of the Spirit of Christ, the spirit of purity, truth and love, and of lowly self-sacrifice for them all. Nay if we turn our eyes to the future, the spiritual imagination, like poetic foresight in its highest mood, sees only in the more perfectly divine Humanity to come, "the Christ that is to be."

### III.

But after all, what is the value of such an element in our nature? I hear some complain that all spiritual perceptions are dim and vague; that religious notions are for the most part incapable of clear definition. To this it is customary to reply that from the nature of the case it must be so. But I am by no means sure about that necessity in the sense in which it is urged. Of course it is far easier to define a triangle than it is to define a conviction of the conscience. But that is only what may be said about the colour red or blue; and for very much the same reason. For the triangle is made up of parts which can be mentioned and their relationship to one another specified; but the colours red and blue are presented to the eye as a confused intuition which can be distinguished from all other objects only by saying that it is—what it is, namely red or blue. The sufficiency of the definition depends upon the sameness of the idea which we and others are accustomed to associate with the words. But a few cases of colour blindness are not thought to justify any complaint about the uncertainty of the idea represented by the words. Supposing the vibratory theory of light to be accepted, it would indeed be possible to define red as a colour, the rays of which vibrate so many thousands of times in a second. But whatever place such a definition might have in a theory of optics, it would not in the least help us in our practical consciousness of the perception of red. I believe that our difficulty in defining some of the intuitions of the God-consciousness may be illustrated by this analogy. For if I say that to speak the truth is right, or to tell a lie is wrong, the sense of right or wrong which accompanies the words is in consciousness—whatever theory may be held about the remote origin of that consciousness—a confused intuition, which is marked to my apprehension only by its difference from all other intuitions; and expressible to others only by saying that it is—what it is, namely, right or wrong. It is a sort of moral colour that I see, and of which I speak to others in the belief, usually justified, that the word recalls to their mental eye the same sensation which I realize myself. The origin of this mental sensation, if I may use the phrase, that is, the process by which God has produced it in man, may very well bear discussion: but no theory on that subject can, or at any rate ought to, affect the nature of the impression that I feel, any more than the adoption or rejection of the vibratory theory of light can affect my perception of red colour. In both cases the theories must be judged by their adequacy to account for the perception. And so with regard to our perceptions of communion with God, of the beauty of self-sacrifice, or our anticipations of immortality, the difficulty or impossibility of defining them can be no proof of their unreality. For they are confused intuitions of dawning spiritual faculties, which we may believe destined to attain fuller powers in another world.

But it may be urged that if we all have the same feeling when we say of one thing that it is right, and of another that it is wrong, yet we differ very much indeed about the actions with which we associate the feeling. And as to perceptions of God in creation or God in the soul, it may be said that even in those who are most vividly conscious of such experience it is so misty and so incapable of verification that it may very well be a mere projection of fancy. Should this notion seem probable, I can only lament that I have been so unsuccessful in exhibiting the place and importance of the God-consciousness in humanity. Here in conclusion I can only suggest, that much of the vagueness and variability which is charged against our spiritual perceptions may be explained if, as just now hinted, the God-consciousness be regarded as an imperfect attribute of the soul, awaiting a fuller growth in the individual and in the race. If the theory of development has any truth in it, we have no right to assume that the generic consciousness of man has attained its utmost stature yet. We are in truth only waking up from unconsciousness; and we cannot tell how men will feel in a fuller consciousness of themselves, the world and God. Even a man who wakes up from sleep in a strange place is often some time before he can bring his perceptions into order, or as we say, collect himself. He sees the walls and windows clearly enough, but his own relation to them and to the living society they suggest is for a time very misty and disjointed. Now such a moment may possibly be analogous to ages of ages in the history of the generic consciousness of man. For what are these amidst eternity? And if there is any law of continuity in past progress from animalism to rationality, from the rule of the senses to speculations of the soul, from self-seeking passion to self-sacrificing love, surely the God-consciousness in humanity has all the promise of the future. Meantime its intuitions may be indefinite, but they are not dim: as our sense of the poetic glory of a landscape is indefinite, not dim. It has the indefiniteness of a boundless splendour which one feels to be dawning more and more. I admit the rapidity with which the glimpses that we get of an Infinite Life are lost in a light that is unapproachable. But I anticipate a day when, as all the colours of the flowers are known to be only imperfect reflections of the sunlight, so that Life shall be felt to be one with all its fragmentary manifestations in creation. I anticipate a day when the God-consciousness shall have such an insight into the universe as to feel that Holy Love is not only God over all, blessed for evermore, but Alpha and Omega, beginning, midst and end. But if you ask, what is that to us who depart we know not whither, while God's dawn is so very faint? I can only urge that the very existence of an individual God-consciousness implies that elsewhere, and in other guise, we shall play our part in the endless revelation. The observations which show that each man in his earliest growth sums up all the progress of the past, and the endless analogies of the macrocosm without to the microcosm within suggest that each individual may repeat in himself the whole evolution of the mystery of God. *"Go thou thy way till the end be; for thou shalt rest, and stand in thy lot at the end of the days."*

Finally, to gather up in briefest compass all that I have claimed for the God-consciousness in humanity. I do not contend that it is a separate and independent faculty; but rather that it is a perception of relationship to God, a perception capable of many degrees of dimness or disguise, and glimmering in the mystic outlook of many higher powers of man, especially of conscience. I maintain that it has been an essential power in all the noblest triumphs of man over self and nature, and next that its very force and essence lies, if not in a clear apprehension of God, at least in its indications of a veiled majesty, such as inspires awe, reverence and love.

When I say the noblest triumphs, I do not mean the bridging of abysses or the levelling of mountains, though these have not been always uninspired by worship: I mean rather mastery over the brute ferocity originally inherent in man, I mean the miracle of orderly society, and the gathering federation of the world. What feeling of loyalty, what bond of brotherhood, what self-forgetful heroism ever ruled or refined the hearts of men apart from some appeal to Heaven? What is said of the great prophet of the Jews is in one sense or other true of every grandest soul the world has ever known—"*he endured as seeing Him who is invisible.*" Enthusiasm and inspiration do not spring from deductions of the intellect. They breathe we know not how—as " the wind bloweth where it listeth," but always from the realms of the Infinite and Divine. A revolution in modes of thought is nothing: the overthrow of an opinionative creed is little—has been accomplished often, and is in course of achievement even now. But the elimination of that adorable mystery, which we call God, from the soul's intensest life and longings would be more than a revolution of thought or creed: it would be the destruction of the generic consciousness of man. For choose what theory you like of conscience, yet your obedience to its voice is prompted by no rational calculation, but by a sense of authority from which no theory eliminates mystery. Make what you will of the physical disproportion between ourselves and the midnight heavens: still it is the inner oneness of the vast expanse, the secret spell of universal Power, which touches the contemplative spirit with awe. Magnify as you may the sweets of intellectual ambition and of gratified human pride; yet the silent rapture which men feel in the sublimest generalizations on substance and on force is something of a purer and a higher tone;—it is as the joy of Moses in his narrow cleft, when he felt the skirts of Jehovah sweeping by. Enlarge as you like on the principle of curiosity in human nature, which magnifies the little cell a thousand times in pursuit after the fugitive life; yet after all, the deepest impulse of this yearning desire to know is the feeling that could we in any single microscopic cell catch the mystery of substance or of life, we should have touched the secret of all that is, we should be translated out of this seeming phantastic world, and should be as gods knowing the eternal good. I care not then what may be said about the variability or the vagueness of this God-consciousness in man. The thing is there. And as the earth cleaves to the sun, as the needle points to the pole, as the rivers often through devious tracts hurry to the sea, so this diviner nature within us cleaves to God, it points to heaven, it pants onward toward immortality.

# LECTURE III.

## INSPIRATION.

*"For it is not ye that speak, but the Spirit of your Father which speaketh in you."*—Matt. x. 20.

PERHAPS no passage in the Scriptures would be more suitable than this, as a starting point for the consideration of the subject which we have now in hand. For that subject is not simply the inspiration of the Bible, though this will naturally occupy a good deal of our attention; but we have to deal with Inspiration in general, of which on any theory the Bible is only a particular manifestation. 'On any theory.' I have said,—because even those, if any, who seriously maintain the 'verbal inspiration' of the Scriptures, and who accordingly regard them as the only instance left to us of this action of God's Spirit on the souls of men, would scarcely insist that all the inspired utterances of prophets and apostles have been preserved. Besides, a comparison of the recorded names of God's messengers to mankind will show that there has been a considerable number of inspired men who so far as we know never left any writing behind them at all.* In a word, the work of inspiration has not on any theory been confined to the production of a book. It has been—and in this lecture I shall contend that it is—a continuous though variable force in the development and progress of mankind. I want us then to understand, what we can only understand by sympathetic feeling, the nature of that experience, half human half divine, which has so gloriously helped our race in its aspirations towards God.

For such a purpose, I repeat, the text is pre-eminently fitted. Its object is not to announce a theory, but to describe a plain practical experience; though like many another plain practical experience, that here described is in its origin and essence very mysterious. "Do not be over anxious," says the Lord to his disciples, already perhaps somewhat fearful at the prospect before them, " never be over anxious about what you shall say when brought before kings and governors; for divine suggestions shall arise in your minds; you shall feel reasons, motives, appeals springing from unknown depths within you; and all you will have to do will be to clothe them in language natural to you; for it is not ye that speak, but the Spirit of your Father which speaketh in you." The mingling of human faculties and divine suggestions is somewhat obscured in our

---

* *E.g.*, Elijah, Elisha, Stephen, etc.

version by the rendering, "*take no thought* how ye shall speak." For what the Lord really said was, "take no anxious thought."\* And when he adds, "it is not ye that speak,"—since it was certainly through their lips that the speech must come,—every one feels that this is an instance of legitimate hyperbole, needed to impress upon the wondering disciples with sufficient emphasis the reality of the divine origination of their thoughts. To the idea of inspiration implied in these words the rough practical conception generally cherished by the popular mind may fairly be considered as corresponding. And in dealing with this subject the popular feeling is most important. For you cannot work out a satisfactory doctrine of Inspiration as you might work out, let us say, the Calvinistic doctrine of original sin, by a consultation and comparison of books. You cannot settle it, as you might the Jewish doctrine of Messiah, by an induction of texts. For it is not a thing of sacred archæology, not a book, doctrine, not a technical link in any rationalistic† theory of the universe. As is well known the word inspiration hardly occurs in the Bible at all; and when it does, it offers no means whatever for determining its significance apart from its appeal to

---

\* μη μεριμνήσατε

† If this epithet describes the tendency to map out the nature of God and the history of his grace so as to make them conformable to technical tricks of human reason, the palm of rationalism must be assigned not to Tübingen but to Geneva.

a general popular conception.* But it is equally well known that the notion of inspiration belongs to what we have recently described as the generic consciousness of man. Our best plan therefore is to realize as well as we can first of all what is the common and essential significance of the notion; then we may illustrate this by some of the most remarkable phenomena which answer to the notion; and in this course we cannot help marking the variations in form and degree of which it is susceptible.

## I.

In seeking what is common and essential in the notion we naturally recur to the derivation of the word. But while doing so we ought carefully to bear in mind that etymology, if a good servant, is a bad master. It generally suggests with wonderful precision the root idea of the word, which idea animates all its later applications. But if we allow ourselves to suppose that the root idea can accurately define or limit these secondary limitations, we are sure to fall into arbitrary pedantry. For example, the root ideas of notorious (well-known) and famous (much spoken of) are very closely akin; but the usage of speech shows that this does not prevent secondary applications of the most divergent and indeed opposite character. In both cases

---

* Whether θεόπνευστος in 2 Tim. iii. 16 be part of the predicate or of the subject this remark is equally true of that passage.

the root idea is suggestive enough as to the meaning of the words; but in neither does it define or limit the application sanctioned by usage. Now the root idea of inspiration is of course 'a breathing in,' as a man breathes into a flute when he plays on it. But if it is argued that prophets and evangelists, being inspired, were nothing but pipes through which the Holy Spirit breathed, and that therefore every word they wrote was directed by God, the error is committed of turning a mere vague suggestion into an exhaustive definition. While however we decline so rigid an application, we gladly adopt the suggestion; for it is very grateful to the spiritual imagination, and will be found, I hope, to fall in with all that was said in our last lecture on the God-consciousness in man.

How often we say of one who has uttered lofty truths with a pure passion that he spoke as one inspired! Such an expression requires no explanation to the common heart. By it we mean of course that in such a case self is subordinate to a great intellectual idea, or to a lofty moral purpose. Such a man is moved by an impulse which is from beyond himself, and which is superior to all selfish considerations. Yet we do not mean merely that he is disinterested. For the disinterested man either feels that self is not at all concerned, or by a candid effort of conscious self-control he puts it on one side. But the man who, as we say, seems like one inspired does not feel anything about self either one way or the other. He is not his own; he is as though possessed by a power greater than his will, beyond his control, vaster than his imagination. This element of spontaneity, of impulse from beyond the range of consciousness, must be constantly kept in view, if we would get a satisfactory notion of inspiration. It does not occur to us to regard as inspired any work that is evidently laboured, patched, hammered together with many a re-consideration and re-arrangement. It is of course quite possible that we may be wrong here. For quite apart from the mere pertinacity of self-will, we see sometimes a quiet earnestness, sustained by an unselfish impulse, and maintaining a patient continuance in well-doing, notwithstanding the utter absence of any facility in performance. When we have any sufficient sympathetic knowledge of such a character we feel, not that the man speaks or acts, but that he *lives* like one inspired. But at present we are trying to get at that popular idea of inspiration, which we believe to have a very strong hold on the generic consciousness of man. And with that object we refer to the phenomena which most manifestly realize that idea. For we naturally think of inspiration as a rushing impulse that comes we know not how, that pours through the soul like a glorious gale, and away out into the world of speech or action, with no strain of effort and hardly a movement of the will. Such a notion may require to be modified or corrected in some instances of its application; but certainly it is a main and distinguishing feature of inspiration as commonly understood by mankind.

Farther, when we say of any man that he spoke or acted like one inspired, we generally imply that his speech or action was characterized by an exalted moral tone. We talk indeed, it is true, of poetic inspiration. But it jars on the conscience to ascribe that to any poetic utterance which is morally bad. There have of course been bad, or at any rate impure men of genius, in whose works we often catch the tones of inspiration. But such utterances have been the impulse of moments when an intense longing after the purity of an ideal life subdued or silenced all baser desires. "Tam O'Shanter" shows the fire of genius; but I hardly think it suggests to one the notion of inspiration, unless indeed in a secondary sense, in which we consciously limit the significance to a free and fervid impulse. Whereas "Mary in Heaven" and the "Cotter's Saturday Night" show that Burns too in a higher sense could speak as one inspired.

In addition, when we use such an expression with most emphasis and in its highest significance, we are impressed with a fulness of life which seems too great to belong to an individual soul. Who does not feel at times in reading Shakspeare as though these could not be the utterances of a limited personal experience, as though some large collective life of many ages and nations must have centred in him, and found expression in his words? They search the depths of the heart; they enlarge consciousness inward, towards the roots of being in which all humanity is one. Nor is such an impression confined to the words of the dead who yet speak, and whose shadowy forms, discerned through the darkness of the past, may be supposed to affect the imagination with a special reverence. For as it is said of those spiritual orators, who perhaps best illustrate ancient prophetic power, that they lose self in their subject; so it is true of their hearers, that in the larger views and deeper feelings realized they forget for a while at least the individuality of the speaker. He becomes to them an oracle, through which for the time they have fuller access to the everlasting Life about us, and the eternal truths which in ordinary moments are so dim and far away.

These then are the notes which make up the idea of inspiration, when in ordinary speech, without presuming to say that such an one *is* actually inspired, we say that he spoke or acted *as* one inspired. We attribute to him possession by a great idea or lofty purpose, a mysterious impulse from beyond self, exalted purity of moral tone, and altogether a fulness of life which seems to break upon us from beyond things seen and temporal. Hitherto we have said nothing of the source of inspiration; because that hardly comes into view in this common and popular use of the word, which we have been trying to describe. That is usually associated exclusively with certain historical experiences of special men. But when we say of any one whom we know, that he spoke or acted as one inspired, this is about what we mean. What then is wanting to enable us to recognize in any instance not a mere similarity, but an actual realization of the idea? Simply a confidence in the true divinity of the impulse which gives a spontaneity beyond any effort of the will. We need to feel that the origin of that impulse is the very life of God, the love of God, the truth of God. And this is just what is expressed by our text, "*it is not ye that speak, but the Spirit of your Father which speaketh in you.*"

Is there anything in this notion of the reality of a divine impulse in the soul to make it an abnormal or unnatural condition of mind? The Christian theory of the universe teaches that God was in the beginning, and will, in the end, in yet a higher sense be all in all. It speaks of "*one God and Father of all, who is above all, and through all, and in you all.*" Indeed I trust I shall not be misunderstood if I say that the Christian theory of the universe has for its background a mystical pantheism: not that it dissolves away the personality of the Most High, or of any of his creatures; but it does seem to imply that God is the only ultimate Substance and the one omnipresent energy of life. And in this its fundamental assumption it has by inspiration anticipated from of old the final issues, toward which science on its own line of enquiry is dimly pointing now, but which by the necessary limitations of its mission science can never reach.\* She tells us that the whole creation is in a state of movement and flux, for ever changing from

---

\* See Appendix, Note D.

glory to glory. Christianity tells us it is "by the spirit of the Lord." As some years ago a myriad meteors burst from one vanishing point in space, and blazed over the whole heaven; so to the contemplative mind beneath the sky of eternity the splendours of creation rush upon the sight; and beyond the vanishing point of vision no eye can intrude: religion only tells us of Him who dwells in light that is unapproachable. To us as Christians there is no beauty, but in it we know that God shines out; there is no life but feels the impulse of his breath; there is no virtue but manifests the energy of his grace. If then we have confidence in the reality of the divine impulse which we regard as the secret of inspiration, there is in our view nothing abnormal or unnatural in this. It is simply a particular application of that theory of the universe which Christianity assumes, and which indeed is the only one that can ultimately consist with faith in God at all.

It may be imagined by many that such a view necessarily does away with everything distinctive in the idea of inspiration, and that in fact we are simply explaining the thing away. But to this I altogether demur. I might as well be told that if I refer to the falls of Niagara as an instance of gravitation, I do away with their distinctive grandeur; or that if I call a flash of lightning a particular manifestation of electricity, I explain away its power and terror. A *particular manifestation* remains a particular manifestation still, to whatever generalization it may be referred.

Circumstance, degree, effect, all have to be considered as well as the ultimate cause. And as I should not think of calling a spark from a Leyden jar a thunderbolt, so I have a perfect right to confine the name Inspiration to special and exalted instances of a divine impulse in human souls. God manifests Himself in the lilies of the field, but we do not call that inspiration; because so far as we know there is here no creature consciousness. God manifests Himself in the strength, and grace, and instinct of the animal world; but we do not call that inspiration, because there is no God-consciousness. God manifests Himself in the laws of thought which govern the operations of human intellect; but we do not call that inspiration, because there is in these no feeling of divine communion. God manifests Himself in answer to every prayerful aspiration, but we do not necessarily call this inspiration—though we nearly touch it here—because there may be no definite impulse, and no distinct overmastering idea. In a word, our idea of inspiration is a divine impulse which takes the form of intense purity of moral feeling, of possession by a lofty purpose, of a fulness of life which energizes in various proportions every faculty of heart and mind. I believe that this essentially accords with the popular idea which we have been seeking to illustrate; but whether the exclusiveness with which the popular notion is usually applied can fairly be maintained, is a question which I at present reserve.

If it is asked how are we to know that the impulse is

divine; I reply, partly by its fruits; partly by the circumstances under which the manifestation takes place. If the issue is an utterance of quickening, elevating, hallowing power, it is quite possibly, though not certainly, a genuine inspiration. "Not certainly" I have said; for if the circumstances are such that surrounding social and educational influences amply account for the utterance or deed, without the supposition of any great originality of impulse, of course inspiration in the highest sense has no place. But if it is impossible to account by such mundane influences for the moral and spiritual power of deeds and words that give men higher life, then we may safely say this is inspiration. A Xenophon or a Euripides, however salutary their teachings, are accounted for if we consider them as instances of cultivated genius; a Moses or a John the Baptist is an incongruous portent if not inspired. We cannot maintain indeed that any man is free from the influences of inheritance and early surroundings. It is in a great measure a question of degree. All we can say is, that making due allowance for this, there are some men who strike us as animated by an original impulse preeminently divine.

But supposing that we are satisfied of the genuineness of inspiration in any particular case, what amount of authority are we to attribute to it? Are we bound to receive an opinion because it has been announced by an inspired man? These are questions which cannot be fully answered apart from a discussion of infallibility, which

I reserve for another lecture. At present however it lies within the limits of our present subject to observe, that according to the idea of inspiration which I have been urging upon you, its force lies in its appeal to the God-consciousness in man. The amount of its authority therefore will depend upon two factors; one being the degree of purity and power with which it passes through the human faculties of the divine messenger into utterance; the other being the amount of attention, susceptibility, and candour in the spiritual nature of the hearers. And these factors are so related that if the one be increased, the other may perhaps be diminished without much difference in the effect; while if one be diminished, the other must be increased, or the authority realized is correspondingly slight. The inspiration which fails to reach the obstinate Jews of Thessalonica is all powerful in the nobler minded synagogue of Berœa. And the Hellenic mind, which can scoff at the *intellectual* fervour of St. Paul on Mar's Hill, yields in Corinth to a simpler and fuller spiritual inspiration.* So amongst ourselves, the inspiration which fails to penetrate self-satisfied irreverent arrogance, brings the moral supremacy of God home to the humble soul. And spiritual natures unsusceptible to the divine impulse beneath the wilder forms of ancient Hebrew inspiration are stirred to repentance and faith by the everlasting gospel of God's love. But this view manifestly puts the responsible relation of individual men to particular instances of

* See 1 Cor. ii. 1, &c.

inspiration, especially to the earthly vessel in which the heavenly treasure is contained, in a great measure beyond human judgment. Indeed I am convinced that could we rightly apprehend the real nature of the authority of inspiration, we should feel opinionative bigotry and sectarian uncharitableness to be impossible, or at least most grossly incongruous with the nature of the case. For the authority of inspiration rests only in the efficacy of its appeal to the tribunal of conscience.\*
And concerning the righteousness of the judgment there the *opinions* of the man are no evidence whatever, one way or the other. His outward life, his manifest disposition may in marked cases be a sufficient indication; but for the most part the purity or impurity of that tribunal is known only to God.

Still, it may be urged, if inspiration has been accompanied by miracles, and if it has risen to the intensity of supernatural visions, not only should its moral influence be commanding, but even the intellectual opinions announced on such credentials must be binding. So far as miracles and visions are necessarily bound up with the present subject, it will be sufficient to reply, that without at all derogating from the import of certain miracles at critical periods of religious history, it may be very safely affirmed that there is no *necessary* connection between any such wonders and the truth of opinions propounded by their worker. No holder of the

---

\* On the submission of personal judgment to the authority of the Bible, see Lect. v.

infallibility of the Bible can possibly dispute this position; because there we find statements to this effect expressly made by Moses, by our Lord, and by St. Paul.* While those who believe in certain miracles on historical evidence, apart from the infallibility of the Bible, are disposed to view them as an extraordinary development of occult powers in humanity, such as might well correspond with an unusual excitement of the spiritual nature. But neither on this view is there any *necessary* connection between miracle and truth of opinion.† Thus the doctrine taught, though it is certainly likely to attract more attention and to come with more weight when accompanied by miracle, must be judged, as we have said that all inspiration is to be judged, by the effect of its appeal on the spiritual nature. And the same principle is applicable to visions. For visions are inspiration in a pictorial form; and in every case that is described in the Scriptures they manifestly owe much of that form to the memory and associations of the seer. But that is only a mode of saying that in this, as in every other form, inspiration issues into utterance under the necessary limitations and imperfections of the individual mind and its surrounding circumstances.

* Deut. xiii. 1—3; Matt. xxiv. 24; 2 Thess. ii. 9. Even the doubtful view that these passages all refer only to pretended miracles would make no difference in the argument; because the works are described as having on the *senses* all the effect of real ones.

† I am aware of two apparently well authenticated events in the life of Swedenborg which were, in the only sense I can attach to the word, miraculous, i.e. altogether beyond the known order of nature. But I do not feel bound to accept his doctrines on that account.

No doubt if we believe that Moses received his account of the creation in articulate intercourse with the Deity, that would be a case in which assent would be a binding duty. But the most devout supporter of such a view would hardly maintain the historical evidence on the subject to be such as to make all differences of opinion impossible unless from depravity of heart. And if there is room for conscientious difference of opinion here, the notion of a binding authority in the theories taught by Moses collapses at once.

There is one other point on which I would touch with all the reverence and love which a devotion at least sincere, though far, far too inadequate can give. For we bless God for One greater than Moses, whose story also stands in a clearer play of historic light. And not only is his Spirit our unfailing inspiration; but his Word remains to us the highest law. Still He speaks to us "as one having authority," and we hear only to obey. 'Is not this then,' it may be asked, ' precisely the case which you seem to regard as impossible? True, "the Father giveth not the spirit by measure unto him," and he stands altogether above apostles and prophets as "the brightness of the Father's glory and the express image of His person." But still his word is not merely an appeal to the spiritual nature; it is also a law imposing on us assent to certain opinions altogether irrespective of any verifying faculty in man.' Even if this were so, it would be strictly consistent with all that we have said on the general subject of inspiration; for by that word we understand *not* a reception of the spirit beyond measure, but *in* measure, and in combination with the ordinary action of human faculties. But though the supreme spiritual authority of our Lord Himself does not in itself come properly within the limits of our present subject, yet its outward action upon us does; because unless in our communion with the Eternal Spirit of Christ, which is of course not outward but inward, the word of our Lord comes to us not directly but indirectly through the gospels, which are on any theory ordinary instances of inspiration. And here I may remark that there is perhaps more significance than is generally felt in the fact that our Lord neither committed anything to writing himself, nor commanded his disciples, so far as we know, to take any memorandum of the forms in which his doctrines were to be taught. Once more we are reminded of St. Paul's most pregnant words, "the Lord is the Spirit;" for the Lord's method in his divine mission suggests that he felt that mission to be, not the authoritative imposition of opinions, but rather the infusion of a spirit into all coming time. Certainly he is said to have promised the apostles that the Holy Ghost should bring "all things to their remembrance whatsoever he had said unto them." But the actual differences amongst the gospels show clearly enough, that this inspiration was subject to limitations involved in the faculties of the individual writers. Still farther, the number of intellectual propositions to which our Lord is reported to have authoritatively demanded an intellectual assent is amazingly small.* The compilers of theological systems have usually had recourse far more to the Epistles than to the Gospels. Indeed the one point on which the Lord does seem to have insisted, the acknowledgment of his Messiahship, was, under the circumstances of the Jewish life of the period, much more a practical matter of the heart than the decision of an intellectual question. All men around him were expecting the Messiah; but only those who were seeking God would recognize, in an incarnation of goodness and love, the long-looked-for salvation of Israel.

We cannot allow then that the exceptional character and mission of the Lord Jesus makes any real exception to the account we have given of the authority appertaining to inspiration. This must lie in the force with which it appeals to the God-consciousness in man. It is mainly a divine impulse giving elevation and intensity to the spiritual life; but the fulness of that life energizes, as we have said, in various degrees every faculty of heart and mind. Insight into religious truth, knowledge of human nature, sympathy with God, susceptibility to heavenly suggestions which no reflection or reasoning could have reached, all associate themselves with such an elevation of soul in communion with the Most High. And these are amply sufficient to account for all the phenomena which are

* Inferences from Christ's use of language and ideas common to the time in which he lived are not in point here; but see Lectures iv. and v.

actually presented by the Scriptures, and possibly by other monuments of the spiritual history of man. I repeat that this view does not explain away everything distinctive in inspiration. It does indeed best accord with that theory of the universe which I have suggested as the mystical back-ground of Christian truth; but it is not to be dissolved away into the generalities of any theory. In the previous lectures we argued that the divine self-manifestation has assumed a special form in association with the gradually awakening self-consciousness of man; that it has in fact become a God-consciousness in the creature, a communion higher than that of the Maker with His works, a communion of the Father with His children, and as such capable of endless degrees of perfection. All we assert now amounts to this, that inspiration is a peculiarly intense form of the God-consciousness in man. It does not belong like that to the generic consciousness of man. It is something special and individual. It is the manifestation of God in the shape of an energy felt, a mission realized, a truth grasped, a fuller wave of life which the enraptured soul knows to be the overflowing of God. That is, to my mind at least, the essential idea of inspiration. And it has this advantage, that it enables us to see in this blessed influence, not a fixed, arbitrary and extraneous force; but a living impulse capable of all degrees, from the higher mind God sometimes breathes on you and me, up through all the ranges of insight, vision and revelation, to the sublimest contemplations of St. John.

## II.

I will now lay before you one or two illustrations, to show how the views advanced apply to acknowledged instances of inspiration. And one most admirably suited to our purpose we shall find in Stephen the first martyr for Christ. If we needed any other evidence of his inspiration in addition to his own work and testimony, we have it in the assurance of the primitive church, that he was "full of the Holy Ghost," in the transfiguration of his countenance by the light within, and in the heavenly vision that accompanied his triumphant death. He was one of the first to experience and to signalize the fulfilment of the Saviour's promise, "*it shall be given you in that hour what ye shall speak.*" And in his speech before the council we shall find the best comment on the meaning of the Lord when he said, "*it is not ye that speak, but the Spirit of your Father which speaketh in you.*" What then are the attributes that most strike our attention in the brief lustre with which this character shines out from the sacred page? At first thought indeed it is hard to say. For the holy passion that consumed him to death, or rather transfigured him into immortality, gives him a sort of single-toned radiance, which makes us conscious only of a longing sympathy with some divine intensity of life, with some unworldly exaltation of motive, some stainless purity of purpose. But if we must examine farther, we should say that the elements which unite in the singular spiritual beauty of Stephen are loyalty of soul, spiritual freedom, singleness of eye, religious insight, and forgetfulness of self in the blessed enthralment of a God-given mission. Of these qualities we may say, not only that they are precisely the elements which make a man an apostle, a prophet or a martyr; but that in such circumstances as make apostleship or martyrdom possible, that is, in formative periods, they are unfailing tokens of an original impulse of inspiration. God shone very brightly in the heart and conscience of this man; and therefore his devotion was not patient only, nor yet exulting, but of that pure calm intensity which we associate with a seraph's joy. He was "full of faith," it is said; and of course it is involved therein that he had clear and definite opinions upon the Messiahship of Jesus. But that does not exhaust the meaning of the phrase. For if you try the effect of this and say, "he was a man full of Christian opinion," you will feel how meagre and inadequate it sounds. No; his soul had embraced with all its powers of self-forgetful affection the divinity that dwelt in Jesus Christ,—the eternal righteousness, the exhaustless love, the reconciling sacrifice, which make the three-fold completeness of the Gospel's manifestation of God to sinful men. It was his complete possession by the spirit of Christ, which gave to this man a loyalty of soul so earnest and deep, so fearless of any change or faithlessness, that in its strength he felt ample liberty to meet new circumstances and fresh needs with new aspects of Christ's truth, in unconventional language fresh from the heart. Nor can we doubt that in this respect he was distinguished above all the earlier apostles, and proved the forerunner of St. Paul, to whom it was finally reserved to break the yoke of Judaism off the neck of the growing church. Neither Peter, nor James, nor even John had yet adequately conceived the utter spirituality of the reign of Christ. They seem to have cherished still the hope that the kingdom should be restored to Israel.\* The paradox of the fulfilment of the law by its abrogation, through the expansion of the spirit beyond the letter, had not yet become an open secret in their minds. There is no evidence that they had any expectation of "changing the customs which Moses delivered," or of making the world instead of their Holy Place the temple of the Living God. In their view the ancient land, hallowed by the very footsteps and echoing to the voice of God, should ever be the imperial province of Messiah's kingdom. As Jews kindled with a more devoted and generous zeal than others, they would have proselytized the whole world; but they could not think that Judaism like a ripened flower must shed its seed and die. That Stephen had already passed beyond this strictly Judaic Christianity is significantly hinted in the accusation made against him, and confirmed by the whole tenour of his apology.† A Hellenist himself,

---

\* Acts i. 6 ; iii. 19—21.

† It is true the witnesses are called false (Acts vi. 13); but so they are in the case of the Lord himself (Matt. xxvi. 61), yet these only distorted, apparently, the actual words of Christ. (John ii. 19.)

and frequenting principally the foreign synagogues which received wanderers from all the earth, he seems to have felt the want of a large catholicity in religion, and to have realized by the sort of insight, which is the peculiar gift of inspiration, that a true catholicity must needs be exclusively spiritual. It may be thought indeed that here one of the conditions of a genuine inspiration is scarcely fulfilled, namely, circumstances suggestive of marked originality. For did not Christ proclaim that his kingdom was not of this world? He did; but the disciples had not generally understood the bearing of his doctrine. And that Stephen alone should have had such an insight into the real nature of the Lord's mission surely suggests a special inspiration by his Master's Spirit. In that inspiration Stephen already knew, what St. Peter himself afterwards learned so well, the freedom that is in no danger of license because it is the spontaneous service of God. There could be no danger in the freedom of such a man, whose cloudless loyalty of soul left no obscurities in the path of duty. The claims of righteousness and expediency never strove together in his heart; for to the singleness of an eye bright with the fulness of his inspired life they were always one. Such qualities, in a soul enriched by prayer and contemplation, always bring with them more or less of religious insight. But if I rightly apprehend the tendency of Stephen's apology, there was in *his* insight just that first look over the mountain ridge barring the way, which always makes an era in the pilgrimage of progress. I think I see those parchment-bound slaves of the letter, those scribes and priests, idolators of a land, a city, a building, a book, as the martyr's face beaming with supernatural light looked back through the centuries past and called them up in vision. What matter that here or there he fell into mistakes of date, or name, or place? The sympathetic souls who saw his face and heard his voice would no more have thought of explaining such errors than of seeking to polish the spots off the sun. And sympathetic or unsympathetic, how strangely transformed, with what a wealth of spiritual suggestion the history unrolled itself before the hearers, searched out by the keen insight of inspiration! Abraham the father of the faithful, an alien and a stranger to the sacred land; Joseph like Jesus, rejected of his brethren; Moses like Jesus, spurned by the people whom he would save; Moses like Jesus, a ruler and deliverer in spite of all; Moses unlike Jesus, the maker only of symbols of heavenly things, the antitypes of which were out of earthly sight;* God refusing a temple made with hands, because enthroned everywhere as the eternal king— such were the flashes of truth which seemed to leap forth from the dulness of the well-worn story, when it was touched by a soul that glowed with the present consciousness of God. In his view the history was a progress from bondage into liberty, from the flesh to

---

* Verse 44.

the spirit, from darkness into light. All through he seemed to hear a divine voice ever "speaking unto the children of Israel to go forward;" all through he could mark a divine hand ever pointing onwards; alike speaking and pointing in vain to the stiff-necked and uncircumcised who would always resist the Holy Ghost. "And all that sat in the council, looking stedfastly on him, saw his face as it had been the face of an angel." Yes; for if anything can make a man's face like an angel's, it is the joy that comes of an inspiration bringing larger views of truth, and impelling to a self-forgetful mission.

Were not the Lord's words fulfilled in Stephen? He was not over-careful to think what he should say. Indeed he had no time. But as the hour demanded, the light in his soul shed its beams over all past history. "While he mused the fire burned; then spake he with his tongue:" and he knew that, however imperfectly, he spoke the purposes of God. Not self-consciousness, but God-consciousness prevailed in him as he spoke. They were not merely the conclusions of experience that he uttered, but the suggestions of the Spirit of God. Therefore it was not only he that spoke, but the Spirit of the Father that spoke in him.

Is not this very much the feeling which St. Paul must have had in writing out of the fulness of his own God-consciousness to sustain and strengthen the faith of his converts? A great deal has been made of a certain passage in the first Epistle to the Corinthians, which is supposed to imply that St. Paul wrote verbatim from the dictation of the Holy Spirit. "*Now we have received, not the spirit of the world, but the Spirit which is of God; that we might know the things that are freely given to us of God. Which things also we speak, not in the words, which man's wisdom teacheth, but which the Holy Ghost teacheth.*"\* In these last words St. Paul has been imagined distinctly to assert, that every word which he dictated to his amanuensis was first dictated to him by a Higher Power. Now I would put it to any candid reader who has given any attention to the style of St. Paul, whether the apostle writes at all like a man who thought every word he uttered was an infallible communication from God? Such a man would surely never argue in support of what he advances; nor would he ever allow himself to be swayed by any passionate impulse. For he who argues expects to prevail not by authority but by reason; and he who is possessed by a passionate impulse is conscious only of a feeling that struggles into imperfect expression, not of facility and perfection such as would be involved in dictation by the Holy Ghost. Such a man would never use forms of adjuration to attest his sincerity, as for instance, "*I protest by your rejoicing*†  which I have in Christ Jesus our Lord I die daily." Such a man would never indulge in biting sarcasm, or in impatient, though most natural wishes which sound like a curse, as for example, "I

---

\* 1 Cor. ii. 12, 13.
† νὴ τὴν ὑμετέραν καύχησιν 1 Cor. xv. 31.

would they were even cut off which trouble you."\* Such a man would not make an express distinction in favour of the authority of well-known moral laws or the received sayings of Christ, as when St. Paul says "to the married I command, *yet not I but the Lord*, let not the wife depart from her husband:—But to the rest *speak I not the Lord.*"† Such characteristics are surely utterly incongruous in any man who is supposed to regard himself as simply an amanuensis to heavenly dictation. No; I think we may give a much more natural interpretation to the passage in the Epistle to the Corinthians, where he speaks of "the words that the Holy Ghost teacheth." For before the apostle was at Corinth he had been in Athens, and he had tried there the effect of such words as man's wisdom might suggest. The speech which he delivered there was a very noble one; but, as I have already intimated, I cannot avoid a feeling that the intellectual interest of the occasion somewhat overbore the simplicity of the spirit. The impulse of inspiration is undoubtedly there, but it is much more embarrassed by self-conscious intellectual effort than, for instance, in the same apostle's address to the elders of Ephesus. He who gloried in being all things to all men desired no doubt to show how the message he had to deliver could be presented in philosophic guise. Nor need we for a moment suppose that there was anything wrong in such a desire; but in that period of sudden regeneration by the marvellous outpouring of

\* Gal. v. 12. † 1 Cor. vii. 10–12.

God's Spirit, the time was hardly suited for its fulfilment. St. Paul appears then to have gone to Corinth in some depression,* saddened by the unimpressionable levity of Athens, and feeling deeply the strange incongruity of the spiritual life he proclaimed with the formalized, polished, and supercilious self-satisfaction of the world immediately around him. And yet when he reached Corinth he could not choose but speak. "Necessity was laid upon him." and silence was a worse woe than the scorn of unbelief. But as he spoke out, in what the Saturday Reviewers of the time no doubt thought barbarous forms of thought and speech, the tale of divine love he had to tell; behold the hearts of men were melted, and their spirits felt the glory of an inner revelation. A sacred excitement spread from house to house; a holy power testified its presence in a moral reformation; and even the sick in body were healed by the strange and sudden grace of God. So says St. Paul, "*my speech and my preaching was not with enticing words of man's wisdom, but in demonstration of the Spirit and of power.*" And this gives ample meaning to the passage which has been supposed to profess dictation from the Holy Ghost. "*Which things also we speak, not in the words which man's wisdom teacheth, but which the Holy Ghost teacheth; comparing spiritual things with spiritual.*" The contrast is not between his own words and the words of another Being; but between words carefully selected in accordance with a prudent intellectual design, as at Athens, and

* Compare 1 Cor. ii. 3.

words rising freely to the lips from a heart full of emotion kindled by the Spirit of God. This view of St. Paul's experience of inspiration could easily be confirmed by a farther survey of his writings.* But for our purpose this illustration suffices. It suggests in St. Paul's case, as in that of Stephen, a general exaltation of the moral nature energizing every faculty, an impulse, an idea, a mission borne in upon the soul by the Spirit of God, but taking form according to the individuality of the man; and this it is which constitutes inspiration.

Bearing in mind what has been said about visions or dreams as a pictorial form of inspiration, we may safely affirm that the ideas hitherto propounded answer very fairly to the ancient prophetic notion of the 'word of Jehovah.' This comes out clearly in a very touching and descriptive passage of Jeremiah,† where the prophet complains of the hopeless burden which his mission seemed at times. "*Then I said I will not make mention of Him, nor speak any more in His name. But His word was in mine heart as a burning fire shut up in my bones, and I was weary with forbearing, and I could not stay.*" Here again we recognize the same experience as in Christian Apostles, an idea, a purpose, a mission borne in upon a man from beyond himself,—the Life of God flowing in upon him with such power as to become practically a resistless impulse. This is a notion of inspiration which amply fulfils the conditions required by popular feeling on the subject: while with

* See Appendix, Note E.  † Ch. xx. 7—9.

due allowance for changes in modes of speech and forms of thought, it is applicable to every genuine instance of inspiration which the world has known.

At this juncture it may be fairly asked, has this experience of inspiration been confined exclusively to the Jews; and are its only records in the Bible? To which I answer, most unquestionably not. For all the tokens of a genuine inspiration, impulse, idea, mission, associated with unusual elevation of moral life, are to be found in some of the greatest heathen teachers; and if you judge inspiration by one rule amongst Jews and make another to exclude it amongst Gentiles, you only reduce it to mere conventional emptiness. Who does not know how Socrates declared himself guided by some divinity within, which animated him with the right impulse at the right moment? And who that has heard or read it does not feel the pathetic earnestness and deep significance of his words when condemned to death, that never had he felt the inward divine indications of duty so luminously clear? How strange —we dare not say capricious—are the issues of the history of faith! It is not Nature only but also Grace that "of fifty seeds" "often brings but one to bear." And while we bless the Providence which has evolved from the old Hebrew consciousness of the Word of Jehovah the glory of Christian inspiration, we cannot but lament that a true Hellenic form of the same doctrine should have wasted into idle jests or idler curiosity about "the Demon of Socrates." One illustration here suffices. It is not necessary that I should give any list of uncanonical writers whom I think to show traces of inspiration. "By their fruits ye shall know them;" the inspired teachers of mankind as well as their followers. Show me the man whose moral and spiritual stature rises above his times, and who earlier than his fellows notes the prophetic tokens of a coming day; a man who by a profound insight discerns, and by heroic faith meets the critical needs of the period; a man who is driven by an impulse, the source of which no reflection can search, to sink all private interests in the ennoblement of human life and the glory of God; and I care not what his creed, his race or his country may be,—there I hail and reverence an inspired man. Let no one fear that acknowledgment of God's work in other races can ever mar the immortal power of the prophets and apostles of the Jews. I do not lower the Alps by calling Snowdon or Ben Nevis a mountain. I do not narrow the Atlantic or Pacific by calling the shallow German sea an ocean. I do not dim the glory of the rose by admiring the daisy and the buttercup as flowers of spring. Is Shakspeare's genius any the less unrivalled because we attribute a sombre majesty to Æschylus, poetic grace to Sophocles, and human pathos to Euripides? No; nor any the more will the supreme spiritual inspiration of the Jewish race suffer any depreciation through a frank acknowledgment of inferior inspiration elsewhere.

Of course if the admission of the reality of inspiration

elsewhere be taken as equivalent to a denial of it anywhere, that is, as merely a mode of explaining it away, I can very well understand the objection which is often felt. But if we heartily insist on the full significance of the word; if we verily believe that God does breathe into the souls of men, and manifest himself in a form higher than any generic consciousness, intenser than ordinary communion in prayer; then surely it cannot lessen the value of the highest inspiration if we admit analogies to it elsewhere. But it may perhaps be asked, as in the days of St. Paul, "what advantage then has the Jew?" What profit was there in the special covenant of circumcision? And the answer given must be the same, "much every way; chiefly because unto them were committed the oracles of God," that is, the records of sacred utterance which preeminently deserve that name. Nor can such language possibly be too strong for the inestimable spiritual privilege, which that nation possessed in its extraordinary prophetic gifts and in the sublime religious tone of its literature. All the difference made by such views of inspiration as we have enunciated is this, that the claim of those ancient documents to be by pre-eminence "oracles of God" is not to be maintained on any abstract or *a priori* theory. Neither will technical tests of authenticity and canonicity suffice. The question with us is simply to what extent do they, like Stephen, make the impression of inspiration on our hearts? With what degree of power do they appeal to, and stir, and brighten the God-consciousness within us? Let no one fear lest the Scriptures should not abide a test like that. Herein is precisely the strength of their hold on human kind, on the generic consciousness, on the common heart of the race. For not one man in a million can estimate the historic accuracy of the story of David, or judge the technical validity of his claims, or those of the other Psalmists, to inspiration. But all can feel the peace that steals over the soul with the words, "*the Lord is my shepherd I shall not want;*" all can perceive the expansive faith of the resolve, "*I will run the way of thy commandments when thou shalt enlarge my heart;*" all can realize the completeness with which the relation of sinful man to God is set forth in the words, "*I have gone astray like a lost sheep; seek thy servant, for I do not forget thy commandments.*" And in proportion to the power with which such utterances appeal to the God-consciousness, will inevitably be the strength of a man's confidence in the inspiration of the writer.

For my own part, unless when pressed by enquirers or compelled by the duties of a teacher, I have never felt any desire to form for myself an intellectual theory of inspiration. But when I have felt the reality of the thing itself breathe like an invigorating air from the pages of the Scriptures, this has been a joy which it is hard for articulate speech to set forth. And I do not know any part of the Bible with which the experience of this joy has been more associated than with the first

Epistle of St. Peter. This does not tell of any great mental gifts; it has none of the intellectual eagerness of St. Paul. But there seems such a quiet deep-toned earnestness about it, such a clear-eyed artless sincerity, such a quick insight into the practical spiritual power and highest use of facts and doctrines, that one can hardly fail to realize in it the direct impulse of God's Spirit. The exuberant thanksgiving at the outset is radiant with heartfelt joy in the higher life which God's grace has given. The appreciative sympathetic communion with Divine Love, shown in all the allusions to Christ; the moral elevation which rises to a tone of grandeur touched now and then with human scorn* in the second chapter; the hallowing light shed on all human suffering from the cross of Christ†—such characteristics as these require no external formulas of sanctity to ensure their appeal to the heart. They come straight home there at once.

Finally, if in this view the Bible should cease to be in the harsher sense a perpetual miracle, on the other hand there are voices in your own souls which at once claim a supernatural dignity. Moses, Elijah, Paul and John—putting aside for a moment external miracles, which are not

---

\* " For so is the will of God, that with well-doing ye may put to silence the ignorance of foolish men "—literally—muzzle the ignorance of fools. (verse 15.)

† " Beloved, think it not strange concerning the fiery trial which is to try you, as though some strange thing had happened unto you: but *rejoice inasmuch as ye are partakers of Christ's sufferings.*" (iv. 12, 13.)

necessarily connected with inspiration—became prophets and apostles through obedience to the same voice that sounds in your own consciences and your own hearts. In proportion as the creature will prevails, and considerations of policy and expediency usurp the tribunal of the soul, so will God seem to be far away, and inspiration an incredible fable of the past. But he that will do the will of the Father shall have experience of this doctrine. And in proportion as expediency and prudence are bowed before the majesty of duty; in proportion as the sanction which touches the conscience with awe is owned to be the supremacy of God; in proportion as we acquaint ourselves with God, and feel that to devout self-sacrifice communion with Divine Love is real and possible; so shall we realize that to contemplative faith all life may be a perpetual inspiration.

# LECTURE IV.

## INFALLIBILITY.

*"Yea, and why even of yourselves judge ye not what is right?"*—
Luke xii. 57.

THERE is somewhere or other in the Government offices a standard yard measure, which is the criterion of all other measures of length used in this realm. And of course by hypothesis it is an infallible test, by which every draper's yard wand and every surveyor's chain may be finally and indisputably judged or corrected. In such a case it is most satisfactory, and indeed absolutely necessary, to have an *external* standard of final appeal, which will permit of no farther discussion or controversy. Similarly men very commonly think that God must of necessity have given us, in some outward objective form, an infallible standard of religious truth and moral right. But in such a mode of argument there is too often forgotten an important element in the case, which has no place at all in the analogy suggested; an element which may perhaps be brought into view by another illustration. I suppose in rifle practice one object in training is to acquire a quick and approximately accurate power of judging distance. For without this, in the field the rifleman would be incapable of accommodating the sights and elevation of his weapon to the required range. And therefore it is the custom in some corps, perhaps in all, to assemble the men for practice in judging distance by naming the range of various objects that may be in sight. Here then, by the very nature of the case, reliance, on the part of the men in training, on any infallible standard is altogether excluded. And why? Simply because the express object of the practice is the education of the power of measurement by the eye. Some hasty unreflecting youth, who did not understand the object, might naturally exclaim, "what fumbling sort of guess-work this is! How much better to stick to a ground already marked out!" Here is in effect a desire to fall back upon the infallible yard measure. But the obvious answer would be, "our purpose is not to inform you what the distance is; but to practise you in judging for yourselves." That, as you see, is an element of consideration which was entirely left out in the analogy suggested just now. Religious and moral truth, say some, is so ineffably important, that to suppose a Government of the universe, which leaves us without any external and infallible appeal in such a matter, is as absurd as to imagine a civilized earthly Government which has no standards by which its subjects can judge their weights and measures. As we shall presently insist, this is very much a question of fact; for it is easier to find out what God has done than to decide what He should do. But as regards the principle involved in such an argument, what we now say is this; that if the office of religious and moral truth is to draw out men's spiritual susceptibilities, to educate the judgment and the conscience, then an infallible standard is precisely what we ought *not* to expect. It is indeed necessary that shopkeepers and surveyors should have access to an infallible standard of length. But that is because there is no question as to the education of their judgment. The measure is a purely conventional thing, which has no existence except so far as it is similarly understood by every one. But now change the case. Suppose that every shopkeeper had not only in his hand a yard measure liable to be corrected by an infallible standard, but also before him on his counter a visible and unerring test of honesty. By a stretch of fancy you may conceive a crystal phial standing by him within view of all, filled with limpid water, which at the moment of any unrighteous dealing should change to blue, or brown, or black, according to the shade of dishonesty involved. This might be very convenient to customers; but it would manifestly do away altogether with the exercise of conscientious judgment on the part of the trader. And as all are in one way or another traders in their turn, the universal application of such an external infallible appeal would simply eliminate the freedom of man's moral nature, and with that its very existence. For nobility of conscience consists not in such agreement with a conventional criterion as can be instantly and definitely detected by the eyes, or enforced by the authority of others; but rather in the refined perceptions which distinguish what coarseness cannot feel; in the purity of tone which elevates the standard, as well as in the loyalty that obeys it. Any thing therefore that dispenses with the exercise of such qualities—and this the establishment of any infallible objective standard must do—necessarily puts a stop to all education of the moral judgment. "*Yea, and why even of yourselves judge ye not what is right?*"

It may occur to some, that while this argument is good enough against the advantage of an infallible *test* of conduct, it is no objection whatever to an infallible *rule* or law, which can only be made a test by the free operation of the individual conscience. But a little reflection will show that a rule, the applicability of which in each separate case can only be decided by the conscience, is *not* an external infallible standard of practice.\* It might indeed be a certain, or if you like infallible declaration of a general truth; as for instance, that it is wrong to steal, or to murder, or to lie. But without saying anything as to the inadequacy of such

---

\* Suppose the imperial yard to be incapable of infallible application except by the conscience of the trader; and it will be seen that it would cease to be an infallible external standard at all.

words to define precisely the wrong that is forbidden, if any one will try to think *why* the thing he feels to be meant by them is in his view so certainly wrong, he will find that it is because of the impossibility of thinking the contrary. That is, the infallibility of the rule lies *not* in the external authority however august which imposes it; but in the resistless assent of his spiritual nature to it when imposed. But it will be said, such an assent is not universally resistless. There are many barbarous tribes who do not think it wrong to murder or steal. Precisely so, I answer; and this only shows that the standard, as well as its application, is a matter of spiritual education. Or as we have already said, nobility of conscience is shown in the purity of feeling which elevates the standard, or in other words, discerns more of God's righteousness, as well as in the loyalty that obeys it. And this purity of feeling is surely best secured, not by the authoritative imposition on unprepared consciences of an infallible general rule in the form of a positive law: but by successive inspirations awakening men's minds to a more and more distinct perception of eternal principles of right. A race in a barbaric state is much more likely to be helped by inspirations that come mingled with and limited by the imperfect notions of the time, than by any infallible exhibition of truth which is necessarily beyond its range. But when that race is educated up to the apprehension of a purer truth, it will need no infallible guarantee. The security of the truth will lie in the impossibility of thinking the contrary.

These observations of course apply mainly, and the last perhaps exclusively, to the apprehension of moral principle. But it may be said, the highest life of man is intimately connected with the apprehension of supernatural or supersensuous facts, such as the being of God, our moral relations to Him, and the immortality which awaits us; all of which are entirely beyond scientific discovery, and absolutely require a divine revelation, if they are to be known at all. Most heartily do I grant this; that is, I believe it quite impossible to explain human history and progress apart from the God-consciousness and the inspirations, which have been the subjects of previous lectures. Through these God has revealed Himself and immortality and heaven to man. These form together the supernatural element in our being, which generates the otherwise inexplicable antagonism, or at least antithesis, of Man and Nature, and raises us into communion with God. In man there is something that we do not know to exist anywhere else in creation—wonder, reflection, hunger after a final cause. And this implies in human history, as distinguished from the physical growth of creation, the introduction of a *new mode* of the continuous creative power; which mode we call grace, divine communion, inspiration, revelation, according to the degree of intensity with which we recognize it. Nor do I know of any really established conclusions which make it irrational to believe that this new mode of the continuous creative power has, like previous modes, had its marked crises of what seems to us special intensity. The doctrine of continuity is probably as applicable to human history as to the geological periods; but in neither application can it be so construed as to exclude any seasons of special activity. And such seasons of special activity we may recognise perhaps in the development of the Caucasian race; perhaps in its separation into the Aryan and Semitic branches; perhaps in the golden ages of imagination which generated their respective mythologies; perhaps in the severance of the Hebrew family from their Chaldean congeners; more certainly in the emancipation of the Hebrews under the sublime spiritual dominion of Moses; clearly in the pure aspirations and impassioned protests of psalmists and prophets; and most plainly in the glorious outburst of spiritual life at the Christian era. At such seasons, even including the earliest, we may believe the minds of men to have been quickened by hints and tokens, or by bright manifestations of higher truth; all of which came from the Spirit of God, from the fuller flow of the life of God into the souls of men. The final cause of all this process we feel must be—if we are capable of apprehending it at all—the elevation of human nature into a nearer communion with God, by the working together of creative grace and creature receptivity in mutual action and reaction. But with such a process the presentation of spiritual doctrines in the form of an infallible* standard for all time is entirely inconsistent. Inspiring suggestions are most precious; glimpses of the divine ideal of life have a glorious power; commands in the name of God arouse us just so far as they can establish their authenticity in the conscience; but the moment these are set up as an infallible yard measure of our thoughts, or words, or deeds, at any rate to whatever extent they are allowed to dispense with the exercise of our judgment, they contravene a manifest and fundamental principle in God's education of the race.

All the remaining remarks I have to make will be more or less an application of this principle. I do not at all forget that, as we said just now, the question is in a great measure one of fact. Has our Heavenly Father, or has he not, seen fit to give us an infallible objective appeal in matters of faith and morals? If he has really done so, the same reasons which made it necessary would also suggest that the fact should be plain and

---

* Possibly some *readers* may think that this involves a denial of the Divinity of Christ. But it really does not. Was the manifestation of Divinity in Christ limited or unlimited? If the former, was it conditioned only by the fact of its presentation in humanity, or also by the specialities belonging to the humanity of a particular age or race? If the latter is the case—and with the Gospel narratives before us it would be difficult to deny it—then it follows that some forms, in which his Divinity was best manifested to that age, have to be dissolved, before we can apprehend their essence. That is, while it is perfectly true, in St. Peter's sense, that the Lord has the words of eternal life, yet he saves us not by his words but by his Spirit; and the Spirit is apprehended by sympathy, not by subjugation to an infallible verbal standard. See Lecture v.

palpable. But in pursuing the question of fact we are likely to be at once less hampered by fear, more reverent and less negative in our treatment, if we keep in view the principles with which we have started. As for my aim, the impression I hope to leave on your minds is this; that while insistance on any external infallible standard is a contravention of the will of God, still in the Bible, in the ordinances of the Church, in the signs of the times, and above all in the communion of our own souls with the divine Spirit, we have amply sufficient guidance to righteousness, immortality and God.

First, then, think of the history of this craving after infallibility; and judge for yourselves what are the indications of God's will which that history suggests. It is of course sufficient for our purpose to trace that desire as it has affected the Christian Church.

It would perhaps surprise many who are conversant only with modern theological discussions, to see how disputed questions are treated by the early Fathers. I remember a debate, somewhat celebrated at the time, in which an evangelical clergyman persisted in interrupting his opponent by calling out "chapter and verse! chapter and verse!" as though the very words were a magic talisman of error. But the early Fathers did not care nearly so much about chapter and verse. At least they did not discuss Christian doctrines with any such exclusive reference to the Scriptures. Their quotations indeed give most valuable indications as to the history of the canon and the sacred text, establishing with considerable certainty the authenticity of most of the New Testament books. Still their mode of dealing with the Apostolic writings shows a feeling in some respects considerably different from that which has been so sedulously cultivated since the reformation. I will try to illustrate what I mean. Papias, writing in the former half of the second century, says that it has never been his habit to care so much for books as for the words that still breathe in living men, that is, he is much more interested in the surviving traditions of the church than in studying any documents whatever. And Eusebius, writing two centuries afterwards, divides the books of the New Canon into three classes; namely, those which were acknowledged by common consent; those which were disputed; and those which were rejected; while one or two books acknowledged by us, and which it is thought a point of our allegiance to the faith to defend, are placed by him, apparently without any feeling that much was involved in the matter, either in the division of the doubtful, or in that of the rejected.* These two references will suggest what might be borne out by many others, that the appeal of the earliest Fathers was not simply to the New Testament, but rather to the testimony and tradition of successive generations in the church. In fact it would not be unfair to say that in their view the church guaranteed the writings, rather than the writings the church. And the New Testament was prized as the voice of the earliest and most purely inspired congregation

\* See Appendix, Note F.

of the saints. The very epithet 'Catholic' shows this; for of course it means simply universal; and the Catholic faith was not exactly that which could be most logically deduced from the gospels and epistles, but rather that which represented a universal and uniform tradition. So one often finds the earliest controversialists counting up the number and exalting the respectability of the bishops who agreed with them, with the evident confidence that should they be able to convict their opponents of transgressing the tradition of the elders, those opponents would be condemned by an infallible standard. I am very far from insinuating that they undervalued the Scriptures. On the contrary, it is not unlikely that they had a more thoroughly sympathetic and therefore more truly noble estimate of them, than those who seem to put the Bible in the place of God. What I do say is this, that on the whole they seem to have prized the New Testament mainly as recording the earliest and most authoritative tradition concerning the foundation and corporate life of the church. And the classification of Eusebius shows that the separate books were themselves submitted to this informal judgment of the church. Most enquirers after infallibility will acknowledge that this vague notion of a Catholic tradition gives a very inefficient standard of appeal. Something of the kind is indeed employed in the English common law: but with the inevitable result of gradual growth and expansion, such as none of our religionists, who at the present day so strenuously insist upon the need of infallibility, could for a moment contemplate with satisfaction. And as a matter of fact crises arose, in which it was felt necessary to define authoritatively what the tradition of the church actually was. With this object Provincial or Œcumenical Councils were from time to time assembled; that is, the Catholic church was summoned to say, by her authorized representatives, what was the truth and life which she enshrined in her heart. The decisions of such Councils, being supposed to sum up the Catholic tradition on the subjects agitated, were naturally invested with infallibility which, if not formally professed, was at least assumed in the claim of implicit submission from all the faithful. The simple words in which the apostles and elders at Jerusalem expressed their confidence that their decision was the issue of divine teaching—"*it seemed good to the Holy Ghost and to us,*"—were taken to justify the arrogance which claimed for the faction fights of wrangling ecclesiastical mobs the infallible guidance and omnipotent control of God's Spirit. But the world changes rapidly; and the interests supposed to be bound up with religious opinion gave a swift impulse to the evolution of thought. Thus the authoritative decisions of one council had hardly been given before a score of new questions were raised, which demanded another appeal to some infallible tribunal for their settlement. But it was impossible that councils on any great scale should assemble very often. And in the mean time the right and duty of private judgment had been so completely overborne or ignored, that each Christian felt utterly dependent on the decisions of the Church. The priests then, being the authorized exponents of those decisions, would become more and more the keepers not only of the consciences but of the intellects of their flock. And as hierarchial authority inevitably involves centralization, the tendency grew up in the Western Church to regard the Pope as the standing representative of an Œcumenical Council, and as invested, for the direction of faith and morals, with the same infallibility. No attempt was made until the present day to define the doctrine in an authoritative form. But as a vague notion, accepted in some undefinable sense by all Romanists, it has undoubtedly existed for long. It is to be feared that those who are most argumentative in their comments on this new 'Papal aggression,' and loudest in their protest against it, are precisely those who fail to perceive the real significance of the revulsion which it is exciting in men's minds. For it is the '*reductio ad absurdum*' of the whole notion of the infallibility which we are discussing. The dogma of papal infallibility is in fact a very logical issue of any real and earnest insistance on the necessity for an infallible standard of truth. For no standard is an infallible rule in practice, whatever it may be in theory, if it is open to various interpretations; and, outside the range of mathematics, this is probably the case with every proposition possible to human language, when the author is not there to be cross-questioned.

What is wanted therefore is a living voice which can give authoritative interpretation to the standards; and that is precisely the office which an infallible living Pope could discharge to perfection. There need be no ambiguity in such a case. If two bishops should differ about the decision of such a Pope, they could refer the matter to him, and ask him point blank did he mean this or that. This now would be *something like* infallibility; and every earnest and sincere insistance on the absolute necessity for a ready and perfect criterion of truth ought logically to involve the need for an infallibility like this.

But the history of infallibility diverged into a new direction at the Reformation. Then it was declared that both Popes and Councils had erred, indeed had been oftener wrong than right; and no ecclesiastical tradition was allowed to have any weight, unless it could be shown that it was not merely primitive but apostolic. Then in the earthquake that shook down the old landmarks, when enquirers eagerly asked what guidance was left for them through the perplexities of their age, they were told that the Bible was amply sufficient for them. Now this was very true; and it was precisely *the* truth which was needed in those times. But I very much question whether some zealous Protestants of our time bear in mind precisely *how* that truth operated on the age of the Reformation. If we would estimate the real value of that teaching, and would rightly judge the direction in which it pointed, we ought to remember what a terrible shaking of the foundations seemed to be involved in the substitution of a difficult book for the plain assertions of Papal authority. I suppose that at the end of the fifteenth century and in the beginning of the sixteenth, not courts and cities only, but families and households were distracted and divided, somewhat as at the present day. "What!" asked the elders, "do you mean to set up your conceited judgment against the venerable authority of the Church and the Holy See?" And doubtless the earnest answer was often meekly given by the young who were thus rebuked, "No, not our judgment; we appeal to the Word of God in the Bible; and *that* we must obey rather than any Pope." Then would come the rejoinder, "But you know that in the interpretation of the sacred Book many learned Fathers have differed much, and have submitted their differences to the decision of the Catholic Church: how can you pretend to distinguish the true meaning, where great men have gone astray?" What reply could be made but this? "We believe that the Spirit, which gave the Word, will enable us to interpret it to the salvation of our souls. Our prayer is like that of the Psalmist, 'O Lord, open thou mine eyes, and I shall see wondrous things out of thy Law.' We may be mistaken in many things; but light enough will be given us to find our way to heaven." Every general reader knows that something like this was the effect of the displacement of ecclesiastical authority by the Bible. It was a movement on the part of the reformers towards freedom, not into another form of bondage; and whatever value might be reverently attached to the Bible, it was in effect an appeal to the individual reason and conscience as illumined by the Spirit of God. How far this was the case may be illustrated by the well-known rashness of Luther; who, because the Epistle of James did not seem to answer to his needs, or at least appeared to contradict those Scriptures which did, rejected it as a thing of straw. We cannot help sometimes lamenting that the course of human affairs should so often have swept aside when approximating to an ideal goal. Like as the children of Israel, when in sight of the promised land, were driven to march back again towards Egypt; so, repeatedly, when in a happy hour some ideal goal of progress was in view, mankind have turned aside, and prolonged their march for a generation or an age. But there has been a meaning and a necessity in it always. The Israelites raw from Egypt were hardly fit to encounter the fierce Anakim so soon. And the Reformed Church fresh from Rome in Luther's days was hardly fitted to grapple with the problems, that must inevitably present themselves on the attainment of perfect spiritual freedom. Hence men turned aside in their march, and had long wanderings in the wilderness which was neither Egypt nor Canaan, neither Rome nor the liberty of Christ. And only at the present day do we their children begin to see some prospect, though remote as yet, of the pure and unfettered life which lives in the Spirit of the Lord.

The old craving for infallibility awoke again as the remodelled churches sought to elaborate their formulas, and were startled by the rapid growth of divergent religious opinions. Nor was that craving left unsatisfied. Just as the Israelites longed for the flesh-pots of Egypt, and were answered by a surfeit of quails which fell in heaps till they bred a pestilence in the camp, so the Protestants, in their Romanist longing for infallibility, were answered by a surfeit of scripture-proved creeds and textual comments on the Bible, which from their day to ours have been at once a satire on infallibility and the source of needless sectarian bitterness. And still, down to the present day, I suppose that a large proportion of the Protestant public would regard the infallibility of the Bible as the Shibboleth which distinguishes the believer from the infidel. It remains therefore that we should address ourselves to a consideration of this substitution of an Infallible Book for an Infallible Ecclesiastical Authority. That for my own part I do so with some trepidation I shall not affect to conceal; trepidation, not from any uncertainty as to the ultimate issue of the opinions I advocate; but from fear lest my words should injure any who have not yet realized the significance of the religious revolution through which we are living; and from a haunting doubt as to how far it is possible for any one, who has gradually grown into particular forms of faith, to help others in suddenly achieving them, without doing violence to the religious life which he only seeks to expand. God forbid that I should say one word to shake the true foundations of any man's faith in God's redeeming love as revealed in Jesus Christ. God forbid that I should in any wise depreciate the Bible as the best source, next to immediate communion with God's Spirit, of the peculiar inspirations that come with Christian truth. But necessity is laid upon us; and woe to those who in these times, through worldly expediency applied to heavenly things, keep back even the faintest glimmer of light which they think they can throw on the present perplexities of faith! If then I speak at all, it is because of an overmastering sense of danger to the faith of the rising generation amongst us and, so far as they can affect it, to that of the coming age, if we obstinately cling to a solemn form of words which has no longer any soul or meaning in it. In this respect an unfortunate and calamitous example is set us by some generally noble leaders of thought, who make no scruple about a solemn declaration that they "*unfeignedly believe all the canonical scriptures of the Old and New Testament;*" to which words no grammatical, common-sense, or real meaning can be given, that is not habitually contradicted by the whole tendency of their influence. The levity of profession and subscription, and the unreality in the use of language, which are unavoidably encouraged by this fast and loose method of playing with the Bible, must surely have a demoralizing influence which the noblest sentiments cannot neutralize. It may be, and indeed probably is true, that the formal nature of such subscriptions and professions makes them more strikingly obnoxious to animadversion; while ten thousand instances of more informal inconsistency escape our attention. But when, in fighting for religious freedom in the open, we are taunted with the special difficulties sometimes found in the narrowness and exclusiveness of free churches—difficulties often ridiculously exaggerated—it is not in human nature to suppress a protest against the intrusion of legal fictions into the divine life in the supposed interests of a liberty which it is well able to assert for itself. Otherwise our protest would be out of place. We should have to search a long time before we found a man without sin in this matter to fling the first stone at the Broad Church Clergy. Many of us, who are bound by no formal pledges on the subject, have yet, in our legitimate anxiety to maintain the reality of God's inspirations and redeeming grace, thought it necessary to insist on the infallibility of the records which embody the history of God's brightest revelations. And under the stress of that supposed necessity we have done violence not only to our own mental faculties, but to the sacred volume itself. Is it not for instance violence which would not be tolerated in dealing with any other record, to import Satan into the narrative of the fall, when no mention is made of any agent but a subtle beast of the field? And what compels us to do so, unless the notion that the comments of inspired men on this narrative give an infallibly true interpretation? Any one, who attends to the unity and internal connection of the sixteenth psalm, must surely feel that to preserve St. Peter's infallibility we do violence to David, when we try to conceive in that psalm any conscious reference to Christ. But if the views advocated in the previous lectures are in the main true, our confidence in God's inspirations and redeeming grace has no need of factitious support from a dogma that has become a mere form. In commencing these Lectures we mentioned, as one of the signs of the times, that it was impossible to state any theory of the Bible's infallibility, without encumbering it with so many limitations as to amount virtually to its denial. But unfortunately very few try to define to themselves what they mean by it. It is sufficient that a spurious peace and rest is given by the decisive ring of the word. Bear in mind what we *should* mean by it if we use the word in its fair and proper sense. Substantial truth is one thing; infallibility is another and a very different thing. Now once more I repeat, I want to loosen no one's hold on the substantial truth of the Bible. Were there any prospect of *that* being seriously threatened, the future might seem black indeed. For that would mean that men were going to lose their faith in the Heavenly Father, their hopes of immortality, and therefore all the higher moral and social forces in which these are essential elements. But infallibility, if it is to be taken in any strict and proper sense, must mean an entire, unlimited, and therefore miraculous freedom from error. Now I do contend that any one who professes to attach this notion to the Bible uses a form of words without any definite meaning at all. For if you ask him is the English version free from error, he will of course have to answer, no; and therefore the infallibility for which he contends cannot reside in that. If farther you ask him does he know of any Greek or Hebrew text that is free from error, he must, at least if he understands what you are talking about, again answer, no. What then *can* he mean by insisting that *the* Bible is infallible? What Bible? He himself never saw a Bible free from error, that is, infallible; nor has he heard of any one else who has. The only meaning then which he can possibly have is this; that the first or autograph copy of each book now bound up in the canon was infallible as it issued from the hand of its particular author. But no one contends that the next scribes, who made copies from each autograph, were miraculously kept from making mistakes; and the separate books were certainly copied out several times before they were gathered into the collection which we call the Bible. Hence it is perfectly clear that no such thing as a really infallible Bible, that is, a complete copy of the Scriptures entirely free from error, ever did or could exist.

The usual answer made to this mode of dealing with the question is of course that it is hypercritical; that it makes a mountain out of a mole-hill: that the mistakes of copyists and translators are altogether trifling, and do not affect any essential doctrine. But how are we to know that? Properly speaking, degrees of infallibility are just as impossible as degrees of parallelism or perpendicularity.

You may say that one pair of lines is more nearly parallel than another; but to say that it is more parallel would simply be an incorrect use of language instinctively corrected in thought. But unless there are definite degrees of infallibility, some one of which can be distinctly guaranteed, how are we to know that in any copy of the Scriptures, or in any Text, there are no mistakes above a certain magnitude? The answer here again is of course that the danger is exaggerated; that any serious undetected mistakes are very unlikely, and that an enlightened criticism shows this to be the case. Precisely so, I reply; but one indispensable element in criticism is the amount of moral probability that this or that should be the original reading; and therefore an infallible outward standard, though once established, lapses after all into an appeal for judgment to "the verifying faculty" in man. Why, what then was the use of that hypothetical, momentary, and miraculous separation of truth from error? We have to separate them as well as we can now; we have to decide, by research and candid criticism, as to the amount of probability that any important errors remain undiscovered. What then is gained by the dogma of infallibility, unless the satisfaction of knowing that the trouble was saved at different periods of history to a portion of some one generation? See then to what an absurdity this notion of infallible writers with erring copyists and translators reduces us. God wrought a miracle to secure in each case an autograph infallible copy of each book, which none but a few scores of people ever saw; but He did not see fit to watch over the preservation of that copy; while every scribe and every translator who afterwards meddled with it was suffered to fall into error. The notion is altogether abnormal, monstrous, incongruous, entirely unworthy of association with the noble history of inspiration.

Thus even on the hypothesis that the writers of each separate book were infallible, to contend for the existence of an infallible Bible now is to use words out of their natural meaning, and in the non-natural sense with which we are unfortunately too familiar. But perhaps it may be said that all our attempts hitherto to represent the doctrine are mere caricature. It may be admitted that no one contends for the existence of any absolutely infallible copy or version of the Bible now. The real doctrine it may be said is this, that whatever statements we have reasonable ground for supposing to belong to the original text we are bound to regard as infallibly true. This we may regard as a moderate statement of the doctrine; the most moderate in fact which is consistent with the retention of any substantial meaning in the phrase "infallible Bible." And in dealing with this we pass over the incongruity between 'reasonable ground' and infallible certainty. When it is remembered what is meant by 'reasonable ground,' how entirely the arguments of textual and historical criticism lie within the compass of the earthly understanding or the merely logical faculties; it will be felt at once that the probability meant by 'reasonable ground' in such a case is entirely incommensurable with the infallible certainty of a spiritual faith which is supposed to be built upon it. But let that pass. We assume it as a fair description of Biblical infallibility, that whatever statements may rightly be regarded as part of the original documents must be accepted as infallibly true. Is it then infallibly true that the earth as it now stands, and the sun, moon and stars of heaven were all created in six days some five or six thousand years ago? As surely as the first chapter of Genesis forms part of the now existing Pentateuch, so certainly was that the simple burden of the writer's story. And the processes of torture, by which every fresh result of geological science has imposed a new interpretation on one of the most unmistakeable and straightforward of narratives, are a striking illustration of the violence which the dogma of infallibility has done to the book it professes to honour. With all the accumulating proofs we have of the very gradual growth of civilization; with our present certainty as to the enormous antiquity of languages widely removed as the Sanscrit and the Basque, together with the long previous development which they imply; with our knowledge that the Negro, the Egyptian, the Chinese, the Aryan existed, in all their diversity of feature, language, and civilization at least two thousand years before Christ; is it possible to regard it as infallibly true that the whole population of the world had been reduced by a deluge to one family some few hundred years before that date? Is it infallibly true that the Almighty Father of mankind made himself a sympathizing partizan in the savage and pitiless warfare of the early Hebrews? Is it infallibly true that He, who is the husband of the widow and the Father of the fatherless, looked on and approved the base and cruel murder of the seven sons of Saul,* nay was appeased, and satisfied, and forewent his wrath when He saw their wretched mother watching in her misery by their gibbeted corpses? "O you must make allowance for the difference of the times," say some; "you must remember that God has been educating the race, and that all these records belong to the imperfect ages of childhood." Good; but that is not the way to treat an infallible standard of historical and moral truth. Truly this would indeed be to play fast and loose with infallibility! Are we to understand that the difference of the times affected the essential nature of the truth, or only the character of the record? If the latter, then this is only a round-about way of saying that the difference of times prevented the record from being infallible. Was it any more true when the Pentateuch was written than it is now, that the universe was made in six days? If that is not the allowance we are to make for difference of the times, the only alternative is that we are to make allowance for the inevitable scientific ignorance of the writer; and then of course infallibility is gone. Or if we are to apply

* 2 Sam. xxi. 1. &c.

the remark to the moral difficulty mentioned just now, since we know that difference of times cannot affect the nature of the Most High, the only other alternative which the difference of the times suggests is a duller perception of the supreme holiness of God. And here again the claim of infallibility is dropped. We are no doubt very rightly called upon to make allowance for the difference of the times. Indeed we ought always to be most anxious to do so; because thus only can we come into sympathizing contact with the struggles of human souls in those days. Studied in this way, the books of the Old Testament are most precious documents, bearing indubitable traces of the divine inspirations which have been the grand impulse of progress. But all *that* remains when the figment of infallibility is abandoned: and abandoned it really is even by those who nominally maintain it.

There is however a notion that infallibility may possibly be confined to moral and spiritual truth. And this would perhaps be maintained by some, who, when the same limited infallibility is claimed for the Pope, would detect the fallacy in an instant. Moral and spiritual truth they would urge do not exist in any abstract state: they are only expressions of relation between man, God, and creation: and whenever any of the terms involved are misconceived, the relations will be more or less misstated. And besides, the method of Scripture, which is like that of Creation, concrete and objective, consisting in evolution of the conscious-self

K

by contemplation of the not-self, is wholly inconsistent with any such separation of the two elements. The lesson, the power, the life are on the whole in the history; and therefore must more or less share the defects of the history. The legendary account of the origin and fall of man naturally lead on to a legendary system of dogma concerning transmitted guilt and the visitation of the parents' sins upon the children, such as will hardly be maintained now to be of perfect purity. Besides, as we cannot allow different degrees of infallibility, the Scriptures ought on such a view to exhibit one continuous level tone of feeling on moral and spiritual life from Genesis to Revelation. But this is notoriously not the case; and the instances already given are sufficient to prove it. Nay, while I gladly admit and earnestly maintain that the New Testament presents us with a most pure and lofty law of life; yet it cannot be denied that here and there notions of morality are taught, which modern Christians quietly ignore as unsuited to their times. Thus the Apostles, in the council at Jerusalem, insisted that abstinence from things strangled and from blood was as much a part of Christian law as purity from fornication; and the complete subjection of women, suggested in the social and domestic ethics of the epistles, is either explained away or openly repudiated now. On the whole then, if the existence of an infallible standard be discussed as a question of fact, it can easily be shown that it is impossible to contend for it as a practical issue at all; that it is merely a sort of pass-word distinguishing rival camps of thought.

But the subject has yet one other aspect, justice to which would require far more time than we have at our disposal. For, as I hinted in my introductory remarks, it is to many minds by no means sufficient to show what God *has* done; but they require us also to show that He *ought* to have done it, and that it is the best thing for us. Well then, if I might presume to justify the ways of God to man, I should urge that successive impulses of inspiration apart from infallibility are best adapted to that gradual progress which God has ordained to be the history of man. Next I would suggest, that reasonable historical certainty concerning the greatest crises of inspiration is all that is needed for the spiritual education of following ages. This gives all the assistance and suggestion and confirmation that a highly developed faith requires, without suffering it to fall into that abject dependence upon the past, which too often seeks the living God only amongst the dead. In support of this point I would remind you, that the direct influence of the Divine Spirit is as accessible now as ever it was to every devout mind. And of course this is in some sort admitted by all Christians, though we cannot but be amazed at the little significance they seem to attach to it. And finally I would insist that our moral and spiritual salvation depends, not on intellectual apprehension of dogma, but on that loyalty of soul which is the essence of all true faith. On each of these points I will say a word to indicate its bearings.

On the whole then we see in the history of mankind a gradual progress from a simpler to a more complex life, from ignorance to knowledge, from narrow superstitions towards a universal religion. Now if in the midst of this slowly growing dawn any sudden flash of absolutely infallible knowledge had fallen on eyes unprepared for such a light, it must have made only a blinding glare, that could only confuse instead of clearing perception. Suppose for instance that Moses, at the remote age when he lived, had been made conversant with the geological history of creation; imagine him to have been taught that the love of God embraces all men of every nation without partiality to any, and that His kingdom is not of this world but spiritual and universal; would not such knowledge have thrown the great prophet wholly out of sympathy with his times, and made him incapable of dealing with a stiff-necked and barbarous people? But feeling only a divine impulse in his soul to raise his people from bondage into freedom, to wean them from idolatry, to inspire them with devotion to the supreme God, to educate them by the wisest laws, and to enrich their memories by the noblest traditions he could collect from the past, this enabled him to serve his own generation so that he became an undying power throughout the history of the world; an undying power, because his constitution and his laws generated spiritual results impossible for him to have foreseen; so that, as the Lord himself said, not one jot or tittle passed from Mosaism till all was fulfilled in a higher form. So is it in all instances of extraordinary influence over the progress of human affairs. That influence was exerted under circumstances which would have made the exhibition of absolutely infallible knowledge an insuperable obstacle to success. Even Christ himself, though so consciously divine, claimed not on earth equality with God. He arrogated to himself no consciousness of omniscience;* nor any supernatural knowledge, except what bore upon the mission He came to fulfil; but meekly lived and died as a strictly human incarnation of divine purity, love, self-sacrifice, in a word, of spiritual truth.

If it be asked how we are to know what He was and did, without any infallible witnesses, I answer that reasonable historical testimony is all we need; and this the New Testament gives us. The misfortune is that if a man denies the infallibility of the gospels, he is supposed to deny their authenticity as well; though there is no necessary connection whatever between the two positions. Their fallacious association in so many minds arises partly, I imagine, from the prevalent exclusiveness of schools of thought, which gather into symmetrical globules like quicksilver dropped upon a table, and know of no communion but complete absorption. Thus it comes to pass that if we adopt a suggestion from any one party, we are supposed to be identified

* See Lecture v.

with it wholly. But the fallacious association referred to arises also from another cause, and that is a distrust, on the part of spiritual conservatives themselves, of the strength of the critical evidences for the authenticity of the gospels—distrust sometimes merely ignorant, sometimes only nervous—but in either case leading to a rash determination to treat the scriptural books in a mode utterly unknown to scientific criticism. For practically it is because of their importance that the infallibility of those books is assumed; and the question of their authenticity is discussed only to give a show of support to this. If then any one abandons the one, he is supposed as a matter of course to surrender the other. At the same time, those who object to the infallibility of the books seem influenced by the same fallacious association to overlook the real strength of the external evidence for their apostolic origin. For my own part, I am strongly of opinion that there are not more than two or three books in the New Testament about the authorship of which there is any reasonable doubt. The quotations in Irenæus, especially considering his connection with Polycarp; the references in Justin Martyr; and the impression made by most writers, whether orthodox or heterodox, of the second century, that the church had grown up under the influence of precisely such an apostolic legacy as we possess in the New Testament Canon, are it appears to me decisive of the question; or at least would be considered so in the case of any heathen philosophers or historians. Even making a larger allowance than I have done for cases of reasonable doubt, still the books\* and the body of apostolic tradition, admitted by all but the wildest prophets of unbelief, form a very strong testimony to the chief events of the Gospel History, including of course the resurrection of Christ. It will be well understood that I am bringing no charge of hardness of heart or wilful blindness against those who think otherwise. I am so convinced of the possible independence of faith and opinion, that I trouble myself comparatively little about the latter. I am only contending that if the events of that wonderful divine sunrise are credible at all, we have evidence enough to prove them; and that if they are altogether incredible, the claim of infallibility for the Book which reports them only recoils upon it, in the addition of undeserved hatred and prejudice to unbelief. All that we need is a consensus of historical testimony strong in proportion to the greatness of the issue; and that I maintain we have in the New Testament books.

The reasonableness of such a position will be more apparent, if we remember that the inspirations of old times were not intended to rob the modern age of direct communion with God: but rather to enrich the nature which makes it possible. They suggest the tender yet solemn responsibility and the immortal significance which underlie the commonest life; and in awakening

\* The Epistles to the Corinthians, Romans, Galatians, and the Revelation of St. John would hardly be disputed by any one.

the conscience they prove, not the possibility only, but the actual reality of present communion with the Father. When once the reality of this is felt, then a criterion of truth is given better far, because more educational in its influence, than any outward infallible standard. For God must be better than the best that we can think: juster and purer than our highest thoughts; more loving, tender, and patient than our compassion's widest reach. Ask, therefore, when other certainties fail, does this or that view of religious truth most enlarge and deepen my love to God and man? Do I feel more the embrace of a Divine Life, when I try to believe in everlasting damnation, or when I "faintly trust the larger hope?" What is most congruous with the most essential conditions of thought and springs of feeling within me, a universe of lifeless atoms, or a world that lives and moves and has its being in God? How do I most worthily think of the Father of my Spirit—as a nameless Abstraction, lonely and apart, or as the glory in the sun, the majesty in the sky, the warmth in the heart, the inspiration of apostles and prophets, "the love of Christ that passeth knowledge?" I know that questions like these may lead to different issues in different men; I know that they afford no rule to ensure uniformity of theological opinion. But if that be made a reproach, it is precisely the difficulty which Romanists, quite as forcibly, make about the substitution of a Book for the authoritative decisions of the Church. And farther, they who make this objection would for the most part themselves deny that any man can read the Bible aright without the help of the Holy Ghost. But if He is our teacher, He needs no *infallible* book to help Him. Nor is it His method to dazzle us with unmixed truth at once. Amidst a world of distracting suggestions, He leads us on from step to step, though in obscurity yet always consciously higher. As when we climb a mountain in a mist, guided by the piercing glimmer of the snow that crowns the cloudless summit, He draws us by His "kindly light," which promises to every aroused and active soul a clearer day, a brighter experience, a higher truth. Keep your face toward the light—in the direction of purer feeling, larger charity, firmer self-control, profounder devotion—keep your face toward the light; for then you are climbing towards God.

Finally, the absence of any infallible measure of theological correctness is not, as some would urge that it is, the slightest derogation from the closely watchful providence and earnest redeeming purpose of God; nor does it make any difficulty in access to His favour: because for this only is man responsible, not for belief of this or that opinion, not for correctness of conclusion, but for keeping his face toward the light; that is, for loyalty of soul. But whenever men urge that God must needs have given us some outward infallible testimony to this or that doctrine because it is so important, there always underlies this assertion an assumption that the knowledge and belief of the doctrine in question is necessary to salvation. But against such an assumption, not the intellect only, but the heart and conscience of humanity increasingly rebel. Yet we freely grant that such a notion could hardly have taken so strong a hold of mankind as it has done, unless it had been a perversion of truth rather than entirely false. What is true in it I believe to be this; that we always need in the future the growing light of some ideal, fairer than anything we have attained. But this ideal, by necessity of the case, just because it is higher and better than any past attainment, is to that extent a revelation of God; and therefore devotion to that is loyalty of soul and faith in God. So Abraham was saved, that is, delivered from base associations, purified, exalted, and made a saint, not by faith in Christ, at least as that phrase is generally understood,* but by faith in the Providence that guided him away from an idolatrous house towards an independent and more spiritual life. He followed an ideal higher than had been attained; and in this he showed the loyalty of soul, which is always in one way or other equivalent to faith in God. So David was saved, not by the meek virtues of a later age, but by truth to the kingly instincts which came as an inspiration from God. So Elijah ascended the heavens of sacred fame in a chariot of fire, not by a creed like that of Augustine or Calvin, but by the ardour with which he followed the high calling of God, in protest against the

---

* But if the words be taken as equivalent to faith in the Love of God, then it is very true that Abraham was saved by faith in Christ.

baseness of the times. Now in the divine humanity of Christ the world received an ideal, which as we believe needs no renewal, save in "the Christ that is to be," the ideal embodied in a race instead of in a man. He breathed upon the world and it arose from death. Since His day it lives a new life, because of the spirit with which He has inspired it. And if there is any failure in the force of our religious life now, it is not a new ideal that we want, but only an expansion of His spirit.

Why should you be alarmed at the responsibility of living in the spirit instead of on the letter? God is with you, God is in you; and because He is with you He asks, "*why even of yourselves judge ye not that which is right?*" He will not condemn you for any intellectual mistake; but only for the disloyalty of soul, which will not follow the guidance of his Spirit towards a higher tone of life and a larger hearted faith. But he who in reverence, sincerity, and self-sacrifice follows the brightest shining of God's light, may feel assured that like the ship with its compass he carries a guide within him, which shall bring him right at last.

# LECTURE V.

## THE USE AND ABUSE OF THE BIBLE.

*"Search the scriptures, for in them ye think ye have eternal life; and they are they which testify of me.*—John v. 39.

As this is our concluding lecture, it will be well to recall your attention to the chief points on which we have insisted in the preceding discourses; because those points are directly suggestive of the remarks I have to offer on the final subject announced. In the first two lectures I asked your attention to certain admitted facts of Human Nature, which imply the absolute necessity of religion for all the ultimate aims of progress; and at any rate make Atheism impossible as the finality of human thought. The longing for a Final Cause, such as can give significance and rationality to the bewildering maze of forces around us, is so ineradicable a characteristic of mankind, that we may well suppose it has some reason in the ultimate reality of things. Some feeling of the Divinity about us is an element in the generic consciousness of the race; and this we have maintained to involve a susceptibility to direct perceptions of God, and to personal communion with the Eternal Spirit. The instinctive reverence which is awakened in the heart by any enlarged view of Creation; the warm loyalty with which the soul recognizes universal law; the feeling of a mystery in life; the prophetic forecaste that this *must* be unfolded more and more, yet never can be wholly revealed—all these are forms of the God-consciousness in man; nay, I believe its signs may be detected in the humblest emotions of wonder, faithfulness, and even curiosity, which distinguish the lowest barbarian from the beast. On the other hand, if the noblest historic experiences of the race, nay if our own highest moments which live in memory mean anything, this sensitiveness to the Divinity which underlies and over-rules the world is capable of becoming a direct and personal communion with God. What then is the food on which this God-consciousness lives and grows? God breathes upon it the breath of life; and in proportion as it is awakened to a realization of its own instincts, it can find God everywhere. But in the weakness and uncertainty of its youth which is not yet overpassed, it most readily and naturally seizes on the inspired utterances of other men and other ages. For such utterances sum up and set in store the accumulated spiritual experiences of days gone by, thus enriching our souls with the concentrated life of great crises in which the progress of centuries bore fruit.

Pursuing this subject in another lecture, we argued that to look for an infallible standard of truth, which can correct the notions of the God-consciousness as exactly as the standard imperial yard corrects the tradesman's measure, is to misunderstand the divine discipline of our souls, and to misread all human history. In this course of thought we have made repeated and special reference to the Jewish and Christian Scriptures, and have endeavoured to show that the principles we have maintained are of necessity applicable to them. As regards their spiritual teaching, we have contended that these Scriptures are supreme but not alone in their inspiration; while we have also endeavoured to show that their infallibility is entirely untenable, and indeed is practically abandoned even by those who strive for the name. The question then naturally arises, what is the right use of the Bible in the cultivation of our spiritual faculties? At the same time the very necessity for asking the question suggests the possibility of abuse; and experience shows that abuse of the Bible has been far too common, with the most mischievous results, not only to religious philosophy, but to piety and morality.

In an attempt to meet such questions, we cannot do better than follow out the suggestions arising out of the instructive and impressive words of our Lord which we have taken for our text. I venture to agree with those who would read those words thus: " *Ye do search the Scriptures, because in them ye think ye have eternal life; and they are they which testify of* me: *and ye will not come unto me that ye might have life."* As it would be out of place to occupy much time now with a point of mere critical discussion, I will content myself with stating in a word or two my reasons for adopting this mode of reading the text. You are probably aware that the verb at the commencement may be taken either as imperative or as indicative. I will not conceal that there is a preponderance of critical authorities in favour of the imperative rendering. Their grammatical reasons for this however are not decisive; and I have a strong feeling that the context not only suggests, but almost requires the indicative. For there was no need to exhort the class of Jews with whom our Lord was speaking to search the scriptures: because in truth they hardly did anything else. Indeed the Lord himself recognizes this in the final verses of the chapter, when he rebukes the hollowness of their confidence in Moses. And when he says, "if ye believe not Moses, how shall ye believe my words?" the argument evidently is, "if you are unimpressed by the preliminary instruction with which you are so boastfully familiar, how is it likely that you can understand my mission?" The indicative would therefore be more consonant with the circumstances and with the following context. But it is also more consistent with the preceding context as well. For in the latter part of the chapter the Lord is referring his opponents to certain testimonies, which they themselves profess to acknowledge. He is not asking them to seek out new witnesses. He is rather urging them to be consistent with the respect or reverence which they profess for those whom they already recognize. He does not say, 'send to John's disciples and ask them what he said,' but, "ye sent unto John and he bare witness unto the truth. . . He was a burning and a shining light, and ye were willing for a season to rejoice in his light." Now since they certainly thought much more of the Scriptures than of John, and were, in their own estimation, much more willing to rejoice in the light of the old prophets than in that of the new, it appears only natural that Christ should add "you are also in the habit of searching the Scriptures; you are confident you have eternal life in them; and they are just God's inspired witnesses for me, to whom you will not come." In that sense then I take the words. And the suggestions I get from them are these: that the use of the Bible is to lead us to Christ, the ideal manhood, the revealer of the Father, the atonement for sin; while the germ of every abuse of the Bible lies in the superstitious attribution to it of any power or sanctity apart from the inspired and inspiring suggestiveness, which is realized only by the Christ-seeking heart. For when the Lord says, "in them ye *think* ye have eternal life," his words are just as much suggestive of a fallacy in the thought, as when he says concerning the heathen "*they think* that they shall be heard for their much speaking."

## I.

In taking up the first part of our subject, which is

the use suggested for the Bible, a preliminary observation or two may be necessary, or at least opportune. For it might be asked, "why take so much trouble about the meaning of the text? On your view of the authority of the Bible, what difference does it make whichever way the words are read?" I might be content with replying, that but for the mode of reading which I have just recommended I should have lost what seem to me to be very fruitful suggestions. But I would rather make some observations here on the nature of the authority of Scripture in regard to moral and spiritual truth; observations, which may supply a needful supplement to what has been said on Inspiration and Infallibility, while they will prepare the way for what must here follow. What I have said about Infallibility is in no way inconsistent with the ascription of a very high authority to the Bible, or with the utmost anxiety for the right interpretation of Scripture; but the authority is necessarily limited and modified by the essential conditions of the case, that is, it is a moral and not a positive authority. In other words, as in effect we said when speaking of Inspiration, there is as much authority as the Word has force enough to carry and as I have susceptibility enough to feel. The objection felt to such a view generally arises from the idea that they who hold it are so filled with carnal pride, that on every possible subject they would maintain their own judgment against the authority of the Bible. But this idea springs from a mistake as to the meaning of moral authority. If a man who has made frequent whaling voyages assures me that whales are often ninety feet long, I submit my own judgment to his knowledge. There is no positive authority compelling me to do so; but there is a moral authority which I have the sense to acknowledge. I may have been of opinion that they are never over fifty feet in length; but when a man whom I respect tells me he has seen them so, I give in at once. If however the same man should assure me that whales are never so long as a hundred feet, because he has never seen one, I do not feel the authority to be so great: and if I have a strong opinion on the point, I hesitate about giving up my judgment, until I know more of the range and length of his experience. It does not follow then, because we ascribe only moral authority to the Bible, that therefore we shall never submit our judgment to it. My judgment, for instance, would naturally be that it is quite impossible for any dead man to come back to life. But I give up my own judgment in deference to the moral authority of men, who certainly testified that they had seen this very thing happen, and whom I believe to have been quite incapable of telling a lie. On the other hand, if the writer of the Epistle to the Hebrews is rightly understood as saying that no Christian who relapsed into deadly sin had any chance of salvation,* I must certainly hesitate to submit my faith in God's love to his denial, because I am by no means sure what opportunities he had of knowing. But the very grounds on which I decline to submit my judgment in this case

* Heb. vi. 4—8.

seem to me to involve submission in the former. Similarly it is a great fallacy to suppose that they who ascribe only a moral authority to the Bible can never feel bound to submit their *feelings,* or affections, or habitudes of mind to its rule. When a parent says to a young child, 'sit up straight:' this is a case of positive authority, in which the judgment of the child has no place, and such an authority as this the Bible certainly cannot exert. But when the Methodist pitman stirred up the members of his little prayer meeting by shouting, "Now lads, shut your eyes and look straight to the Lord," there is no doubt that his exhortation would come with authority of a very different kind. They would feel in effect that this *ought* to be their desire: and however their thoughts might have been wandering, they would realize in the words of their leader a moral authority constraining them to attention. In the same way a clever hasty youth will often feel debarred from rash conclusions about religion, by the moral authority of a spiritual veteran whom he respects and loves; and not only so, but he will be prompted to a desire for the same noble feelings which have moved his admiration. This is the kind of authority with which the words of Scripture often come home to our hearts, "*casting down imaginations and every high thing that exalteth itself against the knowledge of God, and bringeth every thought into the obedience of Christ.*" I have heard of a man whose scornful disbelief of immortality was overcome by the simple words "*thou fool*" in St. Paul's discourse on the resurrection. Nor is such a case at all beyond credibility or understanding. For there is a moral weight in St. Paul's words, such as might very well produce a revulsion from materialistic scicism. I repeat then, it is not true that we who deny the infallibility of the Bible necessarily refuse to submit our own judgment or feelings to its teaching. But in the absence of any positive authority attaching to the book, such submission is necessarily limited to those cases, in which a clearly proved superiority of knowledge, or the home-thrust of some resistless spiritual energy gives a feeling of moral constraint to obey.

Is not this really what is meant when it is said of the Lord Jesus that "*he spake as one having authority and not as the scribes?*"* There are those indeed who insist upon this passage as showing that even in the commencement of his ministry the Lord claimed a positive authority over men's faith, as God's vicegerent upon earth. But the addition of the words, "*not as the scribes*" shows us clearly enough, by contrast, what was the real nature of the impression which Christ's method of teaching made upon the people. For the scribes made their appeal constantly to the positive authority of sacred books or of tradition. But in the teaching of Christ no need of any such appeal was felt. The word came to their hearts carrying its own authority with it. The sense of an extraordinary vigour and impressiveness, requiring no support from rabbinical traditions, would

* Matt. vii. 28, 29.

naturally astonish people who were accustomed to hear every doctrine discussed as though it depended merely on the comparative weight of rival masters. And this astonishment would find most appropriate expression in the exclamation, that "his word was with power,"* or that "he taught them as one having authority and not as the scribes." I believe we are best able to appreciate the feeling of the Lord's first hearers, when we ourselves realize how great is the contrast between the words of our text and the degrading uses to which the Bible is often put in our own times. It is in submission to this authority that we find, in the education of the world and our own souls up to the spirit of Christ, the sole mission of the Bible. I do not of course mean that we take this view as we should accept a legal decision from the positive authority of some final court of appeal. The authority is something nobler in nature than that. The Person of Christ, associated as it is with every pure moral impulse we have known, with every joy of our diviner life—the Person of Christ, from whose feet every spring of modern progress seems to rise, in whose predominance every hope of the future seems to culminate, exercises over our hearts a power of which we are more or less intelligently conscious, and to which we cheerfully submit. The Person of Christ, elevated from age to age by the growing apprehension of his Spirit, abstracted from special limitations of time and place without losing anything of his human tenderness,

* Luke iv. 32.

commends itself to us as the very soul of the divine humanity, the end and consummation of all prophetic longings and apostolic zeal. Hence it is that his word comes to us with power in the utterance of our text; and we find in it a germinant principle, which is capable of ever-widening application, in proportion to men's increasing knowledge of the Bible and their understanding of the Spirit of Christ. The bearing of all this will be plainer as we proceed.

When our Lord uttered the words, or the sentiment, of our text, he was speaking to people who may be said to have worshipped and served the Bible more than the Creator. And were it not for the use—or rather abuse— which is sometimes made of our Lord's occasional references to the Old Testament scriptures, it might be sufficient for us simply to insist on the office which our Lord assigns to the Bible, and to pass on. But in dealing with our text it is of the highest consequence to distinguish between the spirit and the letter. Those to whom the letter is dear will argue with great force, that in these words our Lord himself appears to acknowledge a certain positive authority in the ancient scriptures; and to sanction that sort of Messianic interpretation of ancient prophecy, which almost of necessity involves some infallible dictation from the Holy Ghost. Now as to the first point, the positive authority supposed to be accorded here to the ancient scriptures, a reference to the Sermon on the Mount is sufficient to show that our Lord did not recognize any authority, even in the most sacred words of the Old Testament, which could not be superseded by a fuller manifestation of divine righteousness. *"Ye have heard that it was said to them of old time\* thou shalt not foreswear thyself; but I say unto you swear not at all."* When it is remembered that the command is quoted from Leviticus,† where the words bear the mystic seal of ancient sanctity, in the formula, "I am the LORD," it will be felt that Christ here expressly claims a right to over-ride the positive authority of the Mosaic Law by a revelation of fuller righteousness. His uniform treatment of the institution of the Sabbath implies the same thing. And if he says that not one jot or tittle shall pass from the law till all be fulfilled, the very form of the utterance seems to involve the paradox of fulfilment by abrogation. At the same time it can hardly be denied that the Lord Jesus does so far adopt the customs of the time as to speak in the ordinary manner of generally recognized Messianic predictions.‡ The measureless power of the Divine Spirit in him could not brook the limitations of positive law, where the letter in any degree fettered the life; but it would have been inconsistent with the Lord's special§ ministry to a particular age and race, if he had been unable to make

---

\* Matt. v. 33,34, τοῖς ἀρχαίοις cannot be equivalent to ὑπὸ τῶν ἀρχαίων.
† [...] of the ten commandments is treated in the same way.
‡ J[...] v. 45, 47; viii. 56; Matt. xxii. 41–46.
§ T[...] special in order that it might become general; local and nat[...] as an indispensable condition of its becoming universal. See Matt. xv. 24, x. 5; Acts ii. 25, 26.

a free use of the forms in which the people immediately around him were accustomed to express the spiritual hopes of their fathers and themselves.

While therefore we own and bow before the moral and spiritual supremacy of Christ with a reverence and love which no merely positive authority could command, I think we should totally misunderstand the mission of the Lord if we supposed that it involved the teaching of a scientific system of biblical criticism, or a correct history of the Old Testament Canon. Devout Christians, who know the unanswerable reasons which support, and who mark the resistless tendency of public opinion to accept modern views on the gradual formation of the Pentateuch and the unhistorical character of its account of human origins, must see with pain the practice of setting up incidental allusions in our Lord's discourses as a sufficient reply to the most impregnable conclusions. But this practice is only one of many dangerous results, which spring from the assumption of a dogma usually undefined and never realized, in fact impossible of conception, inconsistent with any true incarnation, and expressly contradicted by the Saviour himself,* I mean the omniscience of Christ. I have always maintained, and I maintain now, that a hearty belief in the essential and conscious divinity of Christ does not at all involve

---

* Mark xiii. 32 ; also, according to the Codex Sin., Matt. xxiv. 36. One such instance is enough to show that the limitation of his knowledge was not, in the Lord's mind, inconsistent with his conscious divinity.

the supposition of his omniscience when on earth. If it did, no real belief in the incarnation would be possible : and we should have to fall back on the phantastic notions of the Docetæ, who regarded the Lord's body as a mere spectral illusion, the arbitrary and empty sign of the presence of a heavenly Spirit. For what the incarnation really means is that God was manifested, not in an abstraction of humanity, but in an individual man who " was made of the seed of David according to the flesh," and therefore was subject in all things innocent to the mental associations of Jewish life. I say 'in all things innocent,' for when the national traditions or institutions, such as 'Corban,' ablutions, or the Sabbath, would have limited the free action of his divine charity in word and deed, the measureless Spirit within him spurned such trammels with sacred indignation. That by a supernatural insight the Lord Jesus knew all that was needed to establish in the world a universal religion, and to reveal the moral bases of divine and human relationship in a ministry of divine life and sacrificial death, is a belief that not only commends itself to the enlightened soul, but is very much a matter of fact demonstrable by evidence. If however you suppose this supernatural insight to involve a knowledge of everything that ever did happen or will happen in all the universe—for omniscience can mean nothing else— and if you then try to imagine such a Being going about as a man amongst men, "hearing them and asking them questions," passing through alternations of joy and sorrow, "tempted in all points like as we are," experiencing all our infirmities so many of which spring from our ignorance, expressing anxiety, subject to paroxysms of spiritual conflict, praying that the cup may pass from him, crying in a horror of great darkness, "*My God, my God, why hast thou forsaken me?*" —you will find not merely that there is a mystery involved, but that the one conception absolutely excludes the other, and that either the one or the other, the conscious omniscience or the real humanity, must be given up. The question is not usually faced by those who adore the divinity of Christ. Nor is this much to be wondered at. For the comfort, and strength, and love, the warm realization of our kinship to God, which comes with a sense of Christ's divinity, is not at all dependent on any metaphysical definition of what is meant by it. And when we reflect on the subject, any searching questions seem to touch so nearly all we hold most dear of God's redeeming grace, that we naturally hesitate to press them. I am not saying how far this is right,—particularly in times when men are everywhere sinking shafts to examine primeval foundations, and when any prohibition of the search seems to imply a fear that there is no foundation there. But whether or not, the feeling is most natural and when unaccompanied by bigotry often even salutary. The point however on which I would insist is this, that before any one sets up incidental allusions in reported words of Christ as a contradiction to conclusions dependent on scientific or critical evidence, he is bound to face this question and to answer it. In fact in using such an argument he assumes an answer, the nature of which he has probably never defined, and the inevitable consequences of which he would certainly abjure. Was the Lord Jesus consciously omniscient or was he not? Supposing that we could so far ignore his own words as to say that he was; then what is meant by calling him a man? Or how could he be tempted in all points like as we are? But if he was not; then how do we know that biblical criticism and sacred archaeology lay within those limits of consciousness which were amongst the inevitable conditions of his mission? There is nothing whatever in his own descriptions of his earthly mission to involve the need for such knowledge; and we have no authority either positive or moral for insisting on his possession of it. There are I suppose those who attempt to meet the difficulty by asserting what in effect amounts to this, that though the Lord was not consciously omniscient, yet he was *unconsciously* so; that is, that every thought as it presented itself to his mind was seen in its absolute truth, and therefore that every word he uttered however incidentally, necessarily implied facts in strict accordance therewith. But to say nothing of the impossibility of knowing anything in its absolute truth unless it is known in all its relations, that is, unless it is viewed as conscious omniscience only can view it; a little reflection would show that this is just as inconsistent as the other notion with participation in human nature and its infirmities. On this theory, as well as on the other, there could be no substantial truth whatever in the thought so dear to Christians that the Lord "was tempted in all points like as we are." For we all agree that he was not exposed to the temptations of a depraved disposition. Now if abstraction be made of this, it may fairly be contended that no point of temptation remains which is not simply the result of our ignorance,\* and in particular of our ignorance concerning some bearings of the matter in hand. By no possibility then can we consistently keep at once the human trials of the Saviour and his unlimited knowledge. Not without deep significance does St. John the Divine reiterate with so much emphasis that Jesus Christ *came in the flesh*. That glorious pathetic life was no mere simulation of our nature, no impossible picture in which practical conditions are ignored. He came in the flesh; He was made under the law. And the veiled spiritual majesty which dwelt in him gives us no right

---

\* A depraved inclination being, *ex hypothesi*, eliminated, it is certain that if we could see things in all their relations as God does, we should choose what is best without any temptation to do otherwise. Our shortsightedness has to be supplemented by faith in God. Even apart from any depraved inclination, it requires a considerable effort of faith to keep on in the path of duty, when all foreseen consequences are against us. Now if all *ultimate* consequences were seen, it would require no faith to do what is right. It is therefore only through limited knowledge that an innocent being can know temptation. But if at any single point the alternative presented is entirely and utterly known in the light of absolute truth, this limitation of knowledge is practically done away.

whatever to expect, that in his forms of thought and speech he should wholly dissociate himself from the mental habits and traditions of his day. I repeat that God was manifested not in an abstraction of humanity, but in individual man, who did not disdain Jewish nationality and Galilean associations, even while consciously the Son of God.

But now in pursuit of our subject, the sense in which the scriptures bear witness to Christ, I must remind you that one main object of the incarnation was to give a more definite idea of a universal Spirit. The words may be vague; yet the significance is *felt* by all who have longed after a true catholicity of religion. It is to this that we are to look in our highest Christian aims, in accordance with the words of St. Paul to which we have so often referred, "the Lord is the Spirit; and where the Spirit of the Lord is, there is liberty." I would apply this principle to our text. The words of the Lord Jesus are often marvellously susceptible both to interpretation in the forms of thought familiar to his own age, and also to expansion by the growth of the spirit which he breathed upon the world. I do not of course attribute to Him, whose every utterance makes so deep an impression of "truth in the inward parts," any cunning device of concealing unpopular esoteric doctrine by a disguise of popular exoteric language. The characteristic to which I refer was simply an inevitable incident of the incarnation of a divine Spirit in a man of a particular age and race. Even words of genius such as Shakspeare's have an ever germinant significance, and constantly find new applications in modes of human life which Shakspeare could by no possibility have imagined. Much more might we look that the incarnate Word of God, speaking in strict accordance with the national and temporal associations of his earthly life, should announce principles which show themselves immortal, though their original associations are dead and buried beyond hope of revival. And so even should it prove that the application which the Jews would make of Christ's words is hardly any longer tenable, it may very well be that there is in the words a wider truth which is imperishable.

It was necessary, in speaking of the one use of the Bible which our text suggests, to premise these remarks, because the more we search the Scriptures, the more are we compelled to acknowledge, that as to the nature of the testimony rendered by the Old Testament the primitive church was very largely mistaken. There are indeed passages, such as the fifty-third chapter of Isaiah, which answer marvellously to the character and work of Christ. Nor can a Christian be wrong in ever keeping that supreme application in view as he reads them. But there is a well-known passage in one of Plato's dialogues, descriptive of the career which would be necessary to prove a love of virtue for its own sake, and showing such a startling resemblance to the general outlines of the life of Christ, nay so nearly suggesting the very mode of his death, that it is just as impossible for a

Christian in reading it to keep such an application out of view, as it is in reading the chapter from Isaiah. Both these voices from the past are in a very true sense prophecies of Christ; that is, they show an inspired idea of what perfect purity, love and devotion must undergo in a world of sin. And in addition, Isaiah sees in this vision of goodness and self-sacrifice a Messenger of God, who may very well have been his divinely suggested conception of the Messiah. But it is as little likely of the one writer as of the other, that he could have had any foresight of the actual and historical ministry of "the Man Christ Jesus." That the Jews had anticipations of a Messiah, which grew more and more exalted as the depression of the nation increased, and as the needs of the spiritual nature were more profoundly realized, no one can dispute. But with very few exceptions, the most startling of these anticipations are found in the post-canonical literature of the Jews, and the number of passages in the Old Testament which can be honestly supposed to have had originally a Messianic bearing is very limited indeed. But the Jews at the Christian era did not think so. Their method of interpretation allowed them to catch at any isolated expressions, which by ignoring the context could be forced into Messianic allusions; and if we were to be bound by the sense which we have every reason to believe they would put upon the words of our text, the only result would be a perilous hold on doubtful predictions, the number of which seems continually to diminish as biblical criticism advances. Besides, the text refers only to the scriptures of the Old Testament; but to us, who are seeking the Spirit of Christ, it suggests the study of the New Testament far more than of the Old. And this shows that as a matter of practice we are actually in the habit of looking at the general principle of the words, disentangled altogether from the immediate application which in the circumstances of that time they would inevitably receive. But the general principle is this, that the scriptures of both Testaments bear witness to Christ; that their divinest meaning is embodied in Christ; that their ultimate mission and the highest blessing they can confer upon us is to lead us to Christ.

Now consider the needs of the God-consciousness, or if you like the phrase better, of our spiritual nature. Like all other attributes of humanity, it needs to be excited, called forth, enlarged by appropriate external objects. And amongst such external excitements nothing perhaps is more quickening than the powerful expression of exalted spiritual experience in others. The same principle is true of all artistic faculty. A sculptor, or a painter, or a poet finds everywhere in nature the objects which stimulate his genius; but yet nature alone would never act intensely enough to educate his faculty, to anything like the extent of its capacity, within the short limit of his life. But from a study of the works of other artists he receives the general influences of nature in a concentrated form; and their action upon his own imagination is correspondingly intense and swift. He must not indeed abandon the contemplation of Nature; but, consciously or unconsciously to himself, the works of art which he has seen are to him the interpreters of Nature; and by their help he passes in the mere infancy of his genius through all past steps of progress, over which his art has painfully toiled during a hundred generations gone. So with regard to the religious faculty; natural religion, as it is called, never yet made a saint. Its operation I suppose to have been slow and gradual, prolonging the evolution of the God-consciousness in man over unmeasured ages of antiquity. But any instance of exalted spiritual experience, especially when it reaches the height of inspiration, may sum up for us the whole divine education of the race. And as Christ is the ideal of divine manhood in this stage of our endless life, every fragmentary inspired hint of that ideal leads to Him.

Thus there is no better food of the God-consciousness in man than its exhibition in men of like passions with ourselves. And this is at least one important source of the quickening influence exercised over us by the worship of the congregation. But to give the whole human race, past, present and to come, the solidarity of one religious life, the conscious impulse of one religious growth, it was needful that there should be a succession of inspired prophets, psalmists, preachers, moralists, whose voices should echo and whose light should shine far beyond the bounds of their own horizon. And towards the accomplishment of this the Bible has certainly done more than any other literature in the world. When I read the words of Moses, *"the eternal God is thy refuge, and underneath are the everlasting arms;"* when I hear of Joshua's manly decision, *"as for me and my house, we will serve the* LORD;" when I catch the strains of David's harp, *"thou wilt show me the path of life; in thy presence is fulness of joy;"* I have a feeling as of a river of life flowing through the heart; a life which is not mine, nor was it theirs; a life too vast for any individual man or nation; a life belonging to the whole race, as it lives, and moves, and has its being in God. This then I conceive to be one of the happiest uses of the Bible; not to teach mere moral maxims which may be found equally well in Confucius or Seneca; not to give an impossible interpretation to mysteries of the third heaven, unlawful to be uttered; but to excite in the soul that sense of life, and love, and joy in God, from which the purest morality and the deepest insight alike proceed. But just in proportion as it does this the Bible leads our souls to Christ. For in him the God-consciousness is deep beyond our sounding line, intense beyond our power of appreciation. And all life, love, joy in God kindle afresh our desires for the incarnate Word who calls us to the bosom of the Father.

Still farther, in these Christian times not only do the scriptures exhibit their highest influence in leading us to Christ, but the peculiar spiritual suggestiveness which has this effect arises to a larger extent than we are many of us aware from the reflected light of the Lord's divine life and death. Divine death! Is that a discord? Nay; his death was, if possible, more divine than his life. The God-nature was never more supreme in him than when he hung fainting upon the cross. For that scene of wickedness, darkness, and horror, the centre of which was a loving broken heart, was surely an expression, so far as that can be given in forms of time and sense, of the mystery of sin's relationship to a righteous and loving Father. Turning from such a scene to the rude simplicity which in the beginning of the Bible declares that in view of the corruptions of the world "*it repented the* LORD *that he had made man on the earth, and it grieved him at his heart,*"* we can feel a significance in these words which their author could not know—a whisper of a possible Divine Sorrow, of a mysterious burden in the Father's heart, such as to our consciences condemns sin more than any flames of hell, while it makes us burn to expend life and all in championship of the cause of righteousness on earth. Thus the wildest dreams of Hebrew legend appear to strain towards Christ. And as in some well-ordered garden all flowers seem to nod with reverence towards one central monarch, all lines to trend, all scents to draw to one midmost mountain of bloom which ends every perspective and pervades the whole air with its

* Gen. vi. 6.

fragrance, so in the garden of the scriptures Christ stands in the midst, the tree of life, with healing leaves and resplendent bloom, dominating every avenue of thought. It is not too much to say that the Lord Jesus merely by breathing upon them has re-written the whole Psalms of David. The words indeed remain the same; but as in a piece of music, the whole strain of thought is raised to a higher pitch by the change of the key note. For temporal dominion we now read spiritual power, for deliverance from enemies redemption from sin, for Mount Zion the Universal Church, for the anointed king of Israel the Christ of God. The very vocabulary is exalted in meaning; the soul, salvation, life, glory, God's word, heaven and hell, all have a more spiritual and therefore an intenser meaning than they could have to David. And so it comes to pass in the providence of God that the Psalmist is the means of suggesting to us thoughts which, could we meet him as he was on earth, he would utterly fail to understand. For our ideal of life is higher, our conceptions of creative Majesty are larger, while at the same time our feeling of divine kinship is more tender and more close than his. It may be said that all this is only the inevitable result of the spiritual progress of mankind. Yes; but we must look at the means by which this progress has been effected; and if we do that candidly, I am persuaded we shall feel that the one event in history which more than any or all others has purified our ideas of God and brought us into conscious nearness to Him is the ministry in life and death of Jesus Christ our Lord. For the gospel story is like a crystal lens amidst converging rays of light which passing through it immediately assume a nobler power. Or rather as, according to some recent astronomical speculations, certain stars drink up, to emit with brighter splendour the nebulous glory that surrounds them, so each dreamy touch of spiritual light and beauty from Genesis to Revelation is first absorbed by Christ before it comes to us, and radiates from him with the power of the whole ideal divine life. And then only do we realize the full spiritual influence which the scriptures are now capable of exerting, when their utterances come to us animated and emphasized by some reminiscence of the divine incarnation and perfect human life which we recognize in Him.

Again, there is a meaning both prophetic and profound in St. Paul's words before Agrippa about "the promise unto which the twelve tribes instantly serving God day and night hope to come." The Jews were but the prophets of humanity. Their longings were the sighs of the whole world's heart. For all aspirations after a purer spirituality, and all desires for a more conscious nearness to God, look towards an ideal of a divinely human life—God in man and man in God—the embodiment of which in Christ is the salvation of the world. Think of David's agonizing prayers for reconciliation; think of Job's perplexity and horror at the apparent chaos of sin and joy, righteousness and suffering.

that seems to brand the constitution of the world with injustice; think of the speculations half expressed half implied in the early legends of Genesis; and the wonder of the prophets concerning the relation of this world's sorrowful and guilty burden to the power and love of God. 'The promise to which all these hope to come' is not merely an ideal human life, but such a a manifestation of God as might make clearer the feelings of His heart towards the world, and especially the relation of His moral government to human sin. The occasional glimpses of some tenderness in this relationship, which flit amongst prophetic denunciations like the sweet sad light that hovers amongst the broken clouds of a gathering storm, are amongst the profoundest forecastings of the Spirit of Christ which the Old Testament ever yields. "*They say, If a man put away his wife and she go from him and become another man's, shall he return unto her again? Shall not that land be greatly polluted? But thou hast played the harlot with many lovers; yet return again to me saith the* LORD."\*
Surely this is an anticipation of a lament diviner still, through which a holy indignation passed into the silence of death; " *O Jerusalem, Jerusalem, thou that killest the prophets and stonest them that are sent unto thee; how often would I have gathered thy children together as a hen gathereth her chickens under her wings; and ye would not.*" " *They shall look on me whom they have pierced, and shall mourn,*" says Zachariah in the name

\* Jer. iii. 1.

of God. And well might John call this to mind at Calvary when all was still. Indeed, apart from all controversy about special predictions, it is most significant that as anticipations of the Messiah grew in wistful eagerness, so they were clothed more and more in the darkness of imaginative woe. In the doubtful touches of such anticipations which gleam here and there amongst the Psalms† the idea is for the most part bright and joyful; the expectation of some king greater than David, under whom the sacred kingdom of Israel should attain all the glory of ancient promise. But Isaiah sees Jehovah's Servant as "a man of sorrows and acquainted with grief." According to Daniel Messiah shall be cut off amidst a sea of troubles. And the pictures of his advent as described in the post-canonical writings of the Jews are often still more gloomy and terrible. When we feel the mystery of the iniquity which abounds in the world, we cannot think that this tendency is without a deep spiritual significance. It shows the God-consciousness in humanity groping towards the truth so grandly expressed in the pathetic and glorious self-sacrifice of Christ. It betrays a dim suspicion that the vital relationship of God and man must first be realized amidst the very deepest shadows of sin. "*If I make my bed in hell*," says the Psalmist,

---

† Under this description I include such psalms as ii, lxxii, and cx., in which some reigning king may have been idealized as the Anointed of the Lord, in such a way as to suggest to imaginative minds some future hope overpassing all past or present realization.

"behold Thou art there." And we, who perhaps feel nearest of all to the suffering Christ when we awake in a great horror of guilt, cannot resist using those words in a sense of which the writer could hardly have dreamt. For the one thing above all others which makes Jesus Christ the power of God unto salvation is the conviction, which he begets in us, that the heavenly Father feels the burden of His children's sins, and that the one awful but most blessed spring of redemption is the self-sacrifice of God shared by His children; or in other words, the cross of Christ taken up and borne by his members. To this all the Scriptures point. For this I prize them most of all; perhaps in this only do they stand unrivalled and alone in the monuments of ancient inspiration; that they awaken our divinest life by giving us to feel that in all our moral conflict, whether for our own salvation or for that of others, we are only taking our part of the measureless burden which oppresses the sensitive love of God. If this then is the testimony to Christ which you value, if this is the inspiring influence which you prize, you may read on undisturbed by rival theories of inspiration; you will be preserved from any desire to make the Bible an armoury for sectarian passion: you may differ from what you think an idolatry of the letter; but you will feel in spirit heartily at one with all past generations of Christians in the love they cherished for the Book of books; because your own soul's experience tells you that the secret of their fervour lay in no opinion that they held, but rather in their devout feeling of what no articles can define, no canons enforce, no intellectual error exclude—"the power of an endless life."

It might be expected that I should here add some remarks on the use of the Bible in the Church, in schools, in the family, and in private meditation. That, however, scarcely comes within the scope of our present purpose, which is rather the suggestion of general principles. But as regards the school and the family, I can scarcely resist the temptation of following up these principles into certain obvious deductions. If the great use of the Bible were the inculcation of moral maxims, or the prescription of rules, which, like those of arithmetic, could easily be called to mind when the conditions of their application arose, then I could well understand the determination with which some insist on making the Scriptures a school-book. But if, as we have urged, the authority of the Bible is moral, not positive; if the purpose of the Scriptures is the inspiration of a divine life and the excitement in the soul of a longing for the Christ of God, then no universal rule whatever can be laid down about the employment of the Book in schools. Very much must depend on the place occupied by the school instruction in the education of the child. Thus if the school be for a while the home of the child, it must, so far as possible, fulfil the offices of home, and provide seasons of gentle, sympathetic, inspiring influence, such as the Bible, read through the living faith of a devout teacher, can so well supply. But if the child goes only to spend four or five hours every day with some skilled instructor, for the purpose of acquiring special branches of secular knowledge, while the real process of education goes on at home, then surely it is better that the school should be content with doing one thing well, and should not lessen the time for its proper duties by attempting what it is quite incapable of performing. Under such circumstances the cases are rare and exceptional in which the reading of the Bible is anything more than the mechanical recitation of a measured quantity of Scripture; a practice not only unlikely to have any inspiring influence in itself, but also exceedingly well-calculated to prevent that influence elsewhere. The associations, the sense of drill, the amount of pressure and hurry, which are inevitable in any large day-school, may be perfectly consistent with a healthy moral tone, and with a reasonable amount of affection between teachers and taught; but in most instances these inevitable incidents are totally incongruous with the *kind* of tone, and with the subtle spiritual sympathy required to enable the Bible to exert its distinctive power. The superstition of bibliolatry is not found practically inconsistent with great levity in the treatment of the Scriptures. And we cannot be far wrong in thinking that the sort of familiar lightness, alternating with conventional but most unreal reverence, which is so very common a treatment of the Bible, is cultivated far more than is generally supposed by turning it into a lesson-book for schools. " When we become men, we put away childish things." The arithmetical rules of the school-room are not those of the counting-house or the bank. The round childish hand, which was the pride of copy-books, is despised by the youth who cultivates the rushing style of a busy man. And when we abandon sum-book, copies, and pedantic grammars, there is great danger that the Bible, if associated distinctively with the class and school, may suffer from the general sense of stiffness and unpractical theory which is connected with all the customs of school. There may be teachers here and there gifted with so fine a tact, and animated by so spiritual a life, that they can make to appear natural in a day-school what would seem absurd and out of place in a warehouse or shop; but they are very few and far between. And till such teachers can be ensured, I am sure that we show the truest reverence for the Bible by leaving it to take its part in education through the family and the church.

By God's ordination, the family is the true nursery of life. The bond of home is strongest and most sacred when it is not merely a fleshly tie, but a spiritual communion; and blessed is that household in which family affections are enriched by the inspirations which hallow them in the love of God. But if, as we believe, the divine life is dependent for its cultivation on the use of the means which God puts into our hands, it is difficult to overestimate the value of family worship in sanctifying the relations of which it expresses the divine ground. No doubt the superstition which regards each scriptural syllable as an infallible utterance of God, and which therefore in daily reading impartially plods through dry chronicles and effete legislature, as well as the still living words of psalmists and evangelists, may here as everywhere else mar the inspiring power of the Bible. But the father or the mother who bears in mind the words of Christ, "*they are they that testify of Me*," will so read the scriptures that their undying music shall at every sunset mingle heaven with earth, and morning by morning brighten with the vision of the divine humanity the daily horizon of life. In after years when the children who knelt together are scattered over land and sea, the memory of those sacred moments will come back; and familiar words on the sacred page will search the heart, and stir the soul, because they fall therein with the cadence of a revered but silent voice. Nor is it parents only who thus ensure an eternal communion with their children. As river communication binds into one realm the snowy mountains and the sunny shore, so the tradition of a divine life is the living rill which most vitally joins "the generations each to each." Never is the grandsire's hoary head so truly a crown of glory as when in the children's memory it is associated with an impressive utterance of the words of eternal life. There are words of scripture which never meet my eyes without recalling the tones of a voice now heard only in heaven, but still echoing in grave musical cadence from the memories of childhood; tones rich in venerable experience, in ripened charity, in all the dignity and tenderness that follow a good fight well fought, and a life's work nobly done. If I refer to personal reminiscences, it is because I am sure I am not alone when I say that the scene which these words bring back is like the gates of the dawn, which the traveller looking behind him beholds afar off amongst the beloved hills of home, if tender with regrets, yet bright with hope, and rich in the promise of life's day. Ah, who can doubt a genuine touch of inspiration in those well-known lines of Burns?—

> "Then kneeling down, to heaven's eternal king,
>   The saint, the father, and the husband prays;
> Hope 'springs exulting on triumphant wing,'
>   That thus they all shall meet in future days:
> There ever bask in increased rays,
>   No more to sigh, or shed the bitter tear,
> Together hymning their Creator's praise,
>   In such society, yet still more dear;
> While circling time moves round in an eternal sphere.
>
> "Compar'd with this how poor Religion's pride
>   In all the pomp of method and of art,
> When men display to congregations wide,
>   Devotion's ev'ry grace, except the heart!
> The Pow'r, incens'd, the pageant will desert,
>   The pompous strain the sacerdotal stole;
> But haply, in some cottage far apart,
>   May hear, well pleased, the language of the soul;
> And in His book of life the inmates poor enrol."

## II.

It is more agreeable to speak of the use than of the abuse of the Bible. Whenever we are driven to say anything about the abuse or perversion of holy things there is a natural disposition on the part of timid souls to take alarm, or at least to question whether it is safe. "*But he that doeth truth cometh to the light, that his deeds may be made manifest, that they are wrought in God.*"\* And "*all things that are reproved are made manifest by the light; for whatsoever doth make manifest is light.*"† Brethren, all honest enquiry and all protest against error are safe so long as we loyally keep our faces towards the light. If there are errors in the Bible itself although its inspirations are so high, much more may we expect mistakes to be made about its right use. That we can infallibly rectify them of course we do not for one moment suppose. But that is no reason why we should withhold suggestions which have even a probable or possible value. And there is great need for the most serious attention to this matter. For while the advance of biblical criticism is teaching the educated classes to value in the sacred volume mainly its power of attraction to "the foundation of apostles and prophets, Jesus Christ himself being the chief corner stone," still amongst the less educated such are the absurd and grotesque perversions of the Bible, that we can only wonder how its more healthy influence has survived at all. Only the other day I noticed in a shop window amongst a number of publications calculated to tempt religious purchasers a pamphlet with this startling title; "the English Nation identified with the Lost House of Israel by seventeen identifications based upon Scripture."

\* John. iii. 21.  † Ephes. v. 13.

In the course of the argument we find that because Isaiah says, "listen O isles unto me," and much else to the same effect, therefore we are to look for Israel upon an island; because Isaiah says, "keep silence before me O islands, and let the people renew their strength," therefore we may look for Israel amongst the 'Saxons' who have very much renewed their strength since they came to England; because Balaam says, "his seed shall be in many waters," and because "many are the references to her calkers and mariners"—I quote the words of the *modern* prophet—"the identity can here be found in an old ballad sung for many years by British tars, to the effect that 'Britannia rules the waves.'" Impious nonsense of this kind—impious not in intention but in effect—may perhaps seem to be unworthy of notice in grave discourse. But it is only an extreme instance of a sort of production which is far too common, and which I suspect would not be so common unless it paid. There seems to be prevalent amongst a large section of the 'religious world' a morbid taste for turning the scriptures into Sibylline leaves, and interrogating them about the ten lost tribes, the fall of the Papacy, the conflagration of the world—anything rather than the Divine Humanity to which they point. The prophets suffer more cruelly from their modern students than from their persecutors: for while some are bent upon sawing Isaiah asunder once more, others stretch him upon the rack of a perverse ingenuity and put him to the question by torture, that they may learn whether the Jews are to go back to the Holy Land or not. It is a sign of a sickly spiritual life, it shows a sad want of any genuine interest in the true mission of the scriptures, when men think to stimulate piety by excitements more proper to the Black Art. Indeed grovelling necromancy of this kind must more or less withdraw the mind from the Bible's noblest influences, and by vain curiosity harden the heart against them.

Perhaps this and most other abuses arise from some such misapprehension of the true place of Scripture as is involved in our text, to which we now revert. "*Ye do search the scriptures; for in them ye* think *ye have eternal life; and they are they that testify of me; and ye will not come unto me that ye might have life.*" Now let us see what is the difference between the man who seeks eternal life in the scriptures and the man who finds it in Christ. The man who thinks he has eternal life in the scriptures looks into the Bible mainly for infallible definitions of doctrine, acquaintance with which or acceptance of which is his salvation. Thus the Pharisaic Jews thought they had eternal life because letter by letter they stuck to the teaching of Moses. So too our Christian Jews appear to think that they are sure of salvation if they can prove that their opinions are identical with those of St. Paul. But the man who looks into the Bible as a record more or less imperfect of the inspirations which have given birth to the divine humanity, seeks that Christ may be formed in his heart; and this, the revelation of God's Son in us, is even now on earth the beginning of everlasting life. Or he who thinks that in the scriptures he has eternal life looks into the Bible for promises made to his own nation, or sect, or opinions. Thus the Jew looked for the promise of a heavenly kingdom which should give the supremacy to his own race. And thus an argumentative Baptist, whom I met once in the street—of course no fair representative of his sect, but indiscreetly zealous for the faith as it is received by them—proclaimed most strenuously that he had sought and found in the Bible a salvation strictly private to the elect members of his own denomination alone; for said he, "it is written in this book, not 'he that believeth' only, but 'he that believeth and *is baptized* shall be saved;'\* now you have no right to strike out the second condition any more than the first; the one is just as necessary as the other." I could not refrain from testing the extent to which it might be possible to carry a sectarian and exclusive appropriation of Heaven, and therefore I joined the wrangling theological circle. "Sir," I said, "you are aware that the overwhelming majority of Christians have been baptized in infancy; is this a sufficient compliance with the condition?" "Certainly not," he replied. "Do you mean to say then that they cannot be saved?" I enquired, thinking that my friend would

\* Mark xvi. 16.

surely be appalled at the tremendous consequences of his creed. "If they die in infancy," said he, as though making a liberal concession. "But," I urged, "if they grow up, and live consistently with their Christian profession, will they not be saved?" "No," said he boldly, "*not unless they are baptized again.*" Now surely this man thought that in the scriptures—in the chapters, and verses, and syllables, and letters—he had eternal life. And whatever may have been his other estimable qualities I maintain that he was far more of a Jew than a Christian.

But he who searches the scriptures for "springs of life" and "seeds of bliss"\* will find by experience of the inward growth of a Christlike nature that he has eternal life in Christ. To look for eternal life in the scriptures themselves is to misapprehend the whole nature and purpose of the Bible. For it is not a volume of sacred incantations, the mere utterance of which can cast out the Devil from the heart. It is not a "*schema de fide*," which we are compelled to hold on pain of an anathema more terrible than the Pope's. It is—we repeat it for the last time—a record of highest thoughts in days of old,

---

\* There is surely both truth and beauty in the lines of Dr. Watts—

"'Tis a broad land of wealth unknown,
Where springs of life arise;
Seeds of immortal bliss are sown,
And hidden glory lies."

an echo of holy voices reverberating in our souls, and renewing in us the aspirations which gave them utterance. Or it is like a constellation, each star comparatively meaningless, but all together marking on the sky of history the image of the Divine Humanity, the Christ of God. Or it is like the bright clouds of dawn, a splendour most touching yet insufficient, strong only to awaken longings which are never appeased till the perfect orb of the Sun of Righteousness rises on the heart, and the Son of God is revealed within. The man, who loves the Bible because through it he meets with men of deep spiritual needs answered by a special inspiration, will be able to judge the scriptures by sanctified reason without the slightest danger of impairing their informing, suggestive, quickening power. Such a man will feel the spiritual inspiration of Moses none the less because he finds the great prophet to have been ignorant of geological facts. Nor, should he be convinced that St. Paul's ideas of biblical criticism fall short of modern requirements, will he any the less testify from his own experience that the Apostle's preaching is still "with demonstration of the Spirit and of power." While acting boldly on the conviction that the Bible was made for man, and not man for the Bible; while steadfastly refusing therefore to ignore any essential instinct of reason or conscience out of deference to ancient inspiration; such a devout student will recognize in the scriptures, probably with more real meaning because with freer loyalty than those who make larger professions, God's great charter of man's freedom from slavery to Nature, God's own testimony to man's kinship with Himself; in a word, the legends, records, and prophecies of the very kingdom of heaven.

In conclusion, I urge, as the one most practical issue of all our thoughts, that if we would find God our Father, we must not seek the living amongst the dead. We must look to present spiritual facts rather than to the ruins of a departed world. Art perishes when it ceases to believe in a still unembodied still unattained ideal glimmering upon the future horizon. Even learning, which treasures up the memories of the past, sinks into a dusty pedantry when it neglects to enrich and inspire by those memories the immortal Humanity, of whose ever ripening experience they are but half forgotten notes. The temples, the cathedrals, the pictures, and the statues of ancient or mediæval genius, are a most suggestive study for the artist now; their office, however, is not to supersede, but to exalt the ideal proper to the present time. The scholar makes a strange use of his Demosthenes or his Cicero when, not content with infusing into English the classic spirit of purity and grace, he seeks to stiffen his native language into classic forms. And surely religion is not less than art or knowledge a power of the present; for it is our life,—our deepest consciousness, our highest feeling, our strongest energy,—the life which we and all mankind live, or may live, in God. When I say that religion is of the Present, of course I feel equally that it is of the Past, as art is of the past, and actual civilization is of the past. It is the now existent moral and spiritual life which has been evoked in the soul of man under the teaching of God's Spirit in many forms. Even as regards the incarnation, I contend that its value to us is the definiteness it gives to an eternal Spirit, and the kinship it reveals between that Spirit and ourselves, oppressed though we are by sorrow and by sin. "God so loved the world;" that is the supreme testimony of Christianity; and however different parties may insist on distinctive views of the atonement, all such views in the end come to this, that "God was in Christ reconciling the world to Himself," teaching men to cry Abba, Father, in the new spirit of sonship breathed on them by the Saviour. Not what once took place, but what now lives and breathes in us is the real work of Christianity for us. We have not denied, we do not deny the serious importance of the relation between the records of inspiration and present spiritual experience. But we do maintain that the question as to the nature of that relation, whether it be one of suggestion or of direct authoritative information, cannot or at least ought not to affect the reality of the life we live in God. At any rate our watchword should no longer be, like that of ancient and modern Jews, "to the Law and to the Testimony;" but rather "the Lord is the Spirit." We own with fervent gratitude and reverence the God-sent gifts which have been handed down to us from ancient days; the enlarged spiritual faculties that have been inherited by us through the accumulated experience of ages; the still breathing inspirations that were sighed forth by broken hearts, or were sounded in trumpet tones by victorious faith. We bow down and worship before that Spirit of purity, love and self-sacrifice, which has verily proceeded from the Father and the Son, that Spirit which is the vital impulse of all true progress. We will study with eager delight, but with patient labour, the suggestive histories of God's prophets and apostles. Above all we will dwell, with a love which no familiarity can exhaust, upon the story of holy flesh and blood for ever luminous with divine truth. We believe the promise given by the Lord Jesus; "*when He, the spirit of truth is come, He will guide you into all truth.*" But if we are exhorted to deny newly ascertained facts because they are incongruous with the forms in which ancient inspirations came, we answer, "the Lord is the Spirit" not the form. If we are urged to look suspiciously upon Science because she cannot pronounce the Shibboleth of old church discipline, we say, she is the child of truth, therefore the sister of Religion; her speech likewise has its inspiration as well as ours. We do not care for old cosmogonies, mythologies, or dogmas, save so far as they add their feeble refracted ray to the growing brightness of God's own dawn. We do not care to stickle for the words and opinions of men, whose worth is measured only by the spiritual impulse which they give to our souls. Let us look to the Bible as God's bow in the clouds of mystery which hover over human life and progress, God's bow bright with broken splendours of revelation; and generations to come shall find it the gateway of life under which they march to a fairer day and a brighter land, where they need no refracted light, because the Lord God Himself giveth them light for ever.

# APPENDIX.

## NOTE A.

*On Buddhism as an Argument for the possibility of rest in Atheism.*

IN the "Theological Review" for April of this year there was an interesting article, by Mr. R. A. Armstrong, on "Buddhism and Christianity," in which the writer seems to regard the former religion, with its long history and numerous adherents, as an overwhelming argument against the natural theism of man. He says (p. 197)—

"This Buddhism exhibits to us not one, but innumerable communities born, bred, dying, without thought or desire of God. It shows us a stupendous power, which has enchained the dwellers over many myriads of leagues without God. It displays a moral empire, which for three-and-twenty centuries has grown and swelled with ever-increasing might without God. It reveals a fortress of rock, against which the waves of Islam and the waves of Christendom have alike beaten utterly in vain,—though the fortress contains no worshippers of God. It manifests a cohesion and endurance which, godless though it be, mocks and shames Christianity with her many convulsions and her reiterated revolutions.

"Therefore to insist that God is naturally revealed to all men, however dimly, is to ignore the largest fact in all history, and to hug a conclusion which is destitute of premises. It may be quite true that we have intuitive sense of Deity, but there are 300,000,000 of human beings in whom that sense is not to be detected."

On this passage I would remark that very much depends upon the sense in which the words "God" and "Deity" are used. If they are used in the full Christian sense of "one God the Father Almighty, Maker of Heaven and earth, and of all things visible and invisible," no doubt the writer's observations are in that case perfectly correct. But then, *mutatis mutandis*, almost the same observations might have been made in the beginning of the fourth century about Teutonic and Hellenic Polytheism. Whatever illustrious exceptions they may have allowed, on the whole these systems showed great vitality, and even moral power, without any notion of God in the full Christian sense. But no one would think of adducing this as an argument against the natural theism of man. If however the words "God" and "Deity" in the above extract stand for "object of worship," the observations are of course notoriously inconsistent with facts. But the writer does not think that worship necessarily involves "theism." Here again everything turns on the meaning of the word. In *our* sense of theism, it certainly is *not* necessarily involved in worship. But it by no means follows that worship is consistent with atheism—at least if that word is confined, as it ought to be, to a denial of any universal, rational and sensitive Life— or what is the same thing, an assertion of the deadness of the universe. If that is the meaning of atheism, I do not think that worship *is* reconcilable with it. The reason why the various deities of a polytheistic system give satisfaction to the instinct of worship is that these deities are embraced by the heart as representatives or impersonations of overruling and abiding Power. This is also the reason why Comtist worship proved impossible; because, as the system ignored any over-ruling and abiding Power, of which therefore collective kindred or humanity could not be taken as the representative, the instinct of worship was not and could not be satisfied. On the other hand, whatever may have been the case with Sakyamuni himself, I understand on the authority of friends born and brought up amongst them and in every way qualified to form a judgment, that the actual religion of the Buddhists is *practically* polytheistic.

Again, if in the above extract the words "God" and "Deity" stand for the Ultimate Mystery of Being, involving both the beginning and the end, the observations made are inconsistent with the traditions detailed in the article itself as to the origin of Buddhism. It was the pressure of the mystery of personal existence which gave to Sackyamuni his first impulse towards the foundation of a new religion. Now what I contend against in Lecture I. is the notion that in delight at the clear and tangible results of physical science men can ever sit down unconcerned about the world's mystery, which of course involves the Final Cause of Creation. It may be true that under the pressure of this mystery Buddhism at the outset took the desperate course of ignoring or even defying it. But the rapid and universal development of its superstitious forms of worship is as good an illustration as I need of the observation I have made that such a desperate course can only be temporary.

The relation of Buddhism to the subject discussed in this Lecture may be suggested in one or two questions and observations.

1. If Nirvana meant simply annihilation, why was not instant suicide conceived to be the nearest way to its attainment? The answer may be that the notion of re-birth or transmigration was too deeply ingrained in the Indian mind to be easily shaken off. But a man who got rid of so much, could surely have found no difficulty in shaking off this. Is it not plain that Sakya-muni realized personality as too deep and intense to be necessarily dissolved with the body?

2. Why should personal existence be singled out as the germ or centre of all evil? Is there not here a hint of the spiritual mysticism which finds in creature isolation from the Universal Good the essence of all sin and misery?

3. If Nirvana was to be attained by purity, self-denial and contemplation, does it not look like absorption more than annihilation? Do not the means for its attainment suggest that originally it must have been regarded as a dissolution of Subject in Object, of self in the Ultimate Good?

I have no knowledge of the sources of information, and therefore cannot pretend to answer such enquiries confidently. But so far as I have learned the facts from authority they seem to point to Pantheism rather than Atheism. In that case they do not necessarily invalidate the principles for which I contend in the Lecture. But such facts concern only Sakyamuni and a few exceptionally enlightened followers; certainly not the 300,000,000 to whom Mr. Armstrong appeals. And therefore I ask—

4. How many of the 300,000,000 differ at all from ordinary Polytheists, in whom superstition satisfies the stunted soul by presenting a degrading object to a perverted instinct of worship?

5. Is not the perpetual succession of Buddhas very like an eternal series of incarnations—of what?

I have been impelled to make these remarks, because I know that some who are interested in the publication of the present lectures are readers of the Theological Review. Those who like myself have to lament their want of information on one of the most stupendous phenomena of history must have felt grateful to Mr. Armstrong for the clear, succinct and candid manner in which he has arranged his facts. It is possible I may be mistaken as to the inferences intended to be drawn from them. At any rate I see nothing in the received facts concerning Buddhism to invalidate, but much to confirm the belief expressed in p. 10 from which reference was made to this note.

As I have quoted the words, I must say I do not at all agree with the sentiment, that "the cohesion and endurance" of Buddhism "mocks and shames

Christianity with her many convulsions and her reiterated revolutions." One might as well say that "the cohesion and endurance" of China "mocks and shames Europe with its convulsions and its reiterated revolutions." The higher the life, the more violent often are the crises of growth, and certainly the more extreme is the differentiation of parts.

## Note B.

*On the Development Theory in relation to the Soul and Immortality.*

On p. 51 I have expressed my belief in the possibility of "a theory of man's spiritual nature, consistent with acknowledged facts, and dependent on no contingencies of any controversy that may yet be undecided." Whether the development of species by some continuous law be an undecided question, I am happily not called upon to determine. But I suppose that one great reason for the repugnance felt to it in years gone by has been the instinctive perception that if it were established as regards animals, it must inevitably be applied to man. And in such an application it is very generally thought that more is at stake than the historical value of Genesis. At the touch of such a theory, if it should be proved, the soul, religion, immortality, must, it is supposed, vanish like a dream. If man was born of a brute, it is insisted that he must of necessity be a brute still. But this of course assumes precisely what the theory in question rejects, namely the constant and insuperable resemblance of descendants to all past progenitors, however remote. For a moment conceive the theory to be limited only to the lower animals. Let us suppose some one to be contending that birds are remotely descended from some form of aquatic animals. What would be thought of any one who insisted that if birds were born of fish, they must of necessity be fish still? It would of course be said that he was talking nonsense. The object of the theory is not to deny or explain away any established facts as to the actual organization of birds, such as the fourfold cavity of the heart, their hot blood, their wings and feathers; but to suggest how the origin of these distinctive phenomena may be accounted for without recourse to the violent supposition of a little heap of dust being suddenly transformed into a full fledged bird. Surely it is not less nonsensical to argue that if the theory of man's remote descent from an anthropoid ape be established, it will prove him to be an ape still. The theory uses the word 'man' in its proper significance, involving intellect, moral nature, and affections, together with all the undeniable phenomena which I have urged as implying a God-consciousness in our race. As the doctrine does not deny the peculiarities of human feet and hands, nor the facial angle, but only tries to account for them; so it does not deny the mental, moral or spiritual attributes which have given mankind supremacy on the earth, but only asserts that they may be accounted for on the hypothesis of development from a lower stage of existence. Whether the theory be adequate to the facts or not, is altogether another question. But if we could only see the theory in its true light, we should not impart so much heat into its discussion.

Still some difficulties remain. One is merely a matter of sentiment. For at first sight it appears abhorrent to religious feeling, that "man who is made in the image of God" should be for a moment conceived as possibly descended from an ape. But is there not something Manichean in such a sentiment? For the lower animals are God's creatures, as well as ourselves. We all feel the truth of the prophet's words to the Jews, "I say unto you, that God is able *of these stones* to raise up children unto Abraham."\* But surely a beast is higher in the scale of creation, and more likely material for such a transformation than a stone. Or the case may be put thus. Both the literal believers in Genesis and the adherents of the development hypothesis alike admit that a material basis was used by the Creator in the formation of man. The former think that "God formed man of the dust of the ground;" the latter believe that the Creator formed him out of an anthropoid ape; or in other words, the former believe that the material basis in the first man, who was "of the earth, earthy," was inorganic dust gathered from the ground; the latter believe that the material basis was dust already organized

\* Matt. iii. 9.

in the form of one of the higher animals. Why the latter view should be more repulsive to sentiment than the former, it would not be easy to say. It is of no use to urge that the material basis in the one case implies something more, viz., that "God breathed into man's nostrils the breath of life." For I maintain that the material basis in the other case implies precisely the same thing, viz., that by "inspiration of the Almighty" man has come to be what he is. It is of no use to reiterate ad nauseam that the scientific men who uphold the origin of man by development are all materialists and atheists. In the first place, it is not true; in the next, I am not at all concerned with their individual opinions, but only with the scientific theories which they seem in a fair way of proving by facts.

Another difficulty is one of more than sentiment. I may be asked how can we have souls if we are developed out of beasts which had none? To which I should reply, I do not pretend to *have* a soul; I *am* a soul. And the collection of phenomena called my body is merely the arrangement of forces necessary, in this present stage of existence, to mark off and concentrate in the form of personality that portion of universal substance which I call 'myself.' This arrangement of forces is the issue of an indefinitely long process of creation passing through innumerable steps. How far the preceding links in the process involved personality, we have none of us any means of determining by direct observation, except for one or two generations. But on historic testimony we believe that the same arrangement of forces, called the human body, has for thousands of years been associated with personality; and when historic testimony fails, we infer from the relics left us, and which bear tokens of personal intelligence, that in pre-historic times this same association prevailed between a certain arrangement of forces and the definition of personal life. That is, every one of the innumerable beings of whom we thus find traces—we do not say *had*, but—was a soul. But when we ask after the ultimate origin of this ever-renewed phenomenon of organic forces, the human body, we are led to believe that it was formed by gradual modifications in a *previous* series of bodies which were no less than ours simply a certain arrangement of forces marking out and limiting universal substance. As then we go back in imagination down the bewildering links of existence till they merge in forms utterly different from ours, we need not look to find the lines of continuity ever broken or disturbed. At every stage creature existence may still be regarded as consisting of two factors; the substance, which is the life, and the defining forces which make the phenomenon of an organic body. Does it then follow that we carry the notion of *soul* with us into every stage? Certainly not. What we mean by that—if we can at all tell what we mean, which is not always the case—is a certain sense of personality, individuality, more or less consciously distinguishing subject and object. Now it is of course common enough to suppose that this sense of personality is developed in the spiritual substance of our being by the education of the senses.

> "So rounds he to a separate mind
> From whence clear memory may begin,
> As thro' the frame that binds him in
> His isolation grows defined."

But it is not the senses only that are concerned in this definition. The senses of many beasts are amazingly keener than ours; but no one supposes that they have any such feeling of individuality as we. If then the "frame that binds us in" "defines our isolation," we must take that frame as a whole, in nerve and brain and blood and muscle, as well as in the senses. It follows that supposing it possible by imagination or knowledge ever to trace the generations of mankind back to a race with an entirely different form of body, or even of brain and nervous system, the attribution of a soul in the above meaning to such a race would be unnecessary and contrary to analogy. The lower animals contemporary with us, quite as certainly as ourselves, consist of two factors, substantial life and phenomenal body. For all the arguments which go to prove the immateriality of human life are quite as applicable to the case of animals. If the difference between living and dead protoplasm involves a subtle spiritual entity present in the one, absent in the other, that spiritual entity is the essence of every animal's existence, as well as of man's. Nevertheless, the popular unwillingness to attribute a soul to beasts is quite justified by the absence of any tokens of that individuality and isolation which we instinctively associate with the word. The probable, or at any rate possible truth is, that the arrangement of forces constituting the body even of the highest animals is inadequate to give that intensity of definition implied in a personal soul. And if the ascending stem of human genealogy blends at its roots with the horizontal stems of animal species, all we can say is, beyond that point we cease to attribute existence in the form of soul. The transition from the one form of existence to the other may be conceived as effected by the gradual perfection of the defining forces which make up the phenomenon of body. There is no need in this case to suppose that the transition must have been sudden. For if personality is the product of a certain intensity in the definition of a part of a universal substance, it is just as capable of gradual development as is bodily form. This may be illustrated by our own personal experience. There is apparently a good deal of truth in the idea, that as we sometimes see each passing wave lined with ripple marks which mimic the surface of the whole ocean, so each individual history is marked by a summary of all the past progress of creation. Certainly there was a time with each one of us when in every respect except in latent power of growth we were mere animals. We have no memory of that time, either because we had no sense of personality or not sufficiently clear; but we know that having once dawned, this sense of personality grew more and more in intensity by action and re-action through means of the body between itself and the world.

I will now try to show the bearing of these remarks on immortality. Here at least it may be thought is an aspect of the spiritual nature which is necessarily dependent on the contingencies of scientific controversy. Were all the lower progenitors of man immortal? If not, when did they begin to be so? And how is such a stupendous transition consistent with the continuity which science is seeking to associate with development? In attempting to suggest an answer to such questions it will of course be understood that I am not dealing with the question of immortality on its own grounds, but only with the relation of the development theory thereto. For those who attach no import to the instinct of immortality within us what I have to say may have little force. But for those who, while believing in immortality, are perplexed by what they think the threatening aspects of physical enquiry, I trust my suggestions may not be altogether valueless. Immortality is one of those "truths which never can be proved," and perhaps pre-eminently requires "the faith that comes of self-control." We who on historical evidence believe in the historical resurrection of Christ may derive from that event great comfort, and confirmation of our faith. But we value it as a confirmation of arguments already existing in our own souls, or rather in the generic consciousness of the race; not as a first revelation, nor as an isolated proof of immortality. Be that as it may, the belief in a future life is one of the most remarkable and surely most significant characteristics of human nature. But now, say some, if the development theory is applied to mankind there is an end to our hope of immortality. I suppose if the precise difficulty is pressed for, it might be presented somewhat thus :—

"If we are immortal and our remote progenitors were not, there must have been a time when the transition was made. That is, it came to pass at some period in the history of development that a mortal father begot an immortal son. There is no alternative. Either a creature is immortal, or he is not. Here is a transition which you cannot bridge over by any graduated process. Therefore you must believe that up to a certain point all the human or quasi-human race were annihilated when they died; and then suddenly the next generation began to live for ever. Is not this on the face of it absurd? Is it not quite as great a miracle as any act of instantaneous creation? Is it not totally inconsistent with the boasted law of continuity?"

I hope I state fairly the difficulty which many may feel as to the bearing of the theory of development on the doctrine of immortality. That I can completely remove the difficulty I do not for a moment suppose; for I believe it to be only one aspect of the one comprehensive mystery involved in the relationship of finite self-conscious life to the Infinite One who is its only true Substance. But something is done if we show that no *new* difficulty is introduced; that it is in fact very closely analogous to an old one which has never, so far as I am aware, seriously disturbed men's confidence in immortality. I spoke just now of the notion that each individual in his own life sums up the past progress of creation. It may be of some assistance by way of analogy here. Are all human offspring from the very moment of conception immortal? I hardly think that any one, however zealous for the proper immortality of man, would maintain this. Or at any rate it is a very exceptional opinion. The ordinary view certainly is that the first beginnings of the individual life do not involve immortality, and that when such an incipient, merely germinant life deceases, it perishes utterly. For myself, I do not believe that it perishes utterly: nothing does; but let that pass for the present. Now at what stage of growth, according to the ordinary view, does immortality begin to be a proper attribute of the individual? Putting aside all old wives' fables, which imply that the soul is a sort of foreign entity inserted by a miracle into the human creature after he has begun to be, is it not felt to be an impossibility to assign any date to this momentous transition? Still if he is to become immortal at all there must be such a period. That is, if he died one moment before a certain time he would be annihilated; whereas if he survives a moment longer he will live for ever. Here you have in the individual history precisely the difficulty above suggested in the relation of the development theory to immortality. Is not this, it might be asked, absurd on the face of it? Is it not totally inconsistent with that continuity of organic growth, upon which all common sense doctrines concerning the nurture of the earliest springs of life are founded? Yet ordinary Christians, strong in the instinct of immortality, quietly ignore any such difficulty; or if they ever think of it are content with a confidence that there must be *some* way out of it. Far be it for me to say that they act unwisely; but it is not open to the same men on account of a precisely analogous difficulty to declare that the development theory is subversive of immortality.

But though the production of a parallel difficulty notoriously ignored may be a sufficient argument *ad hominem*, it is not sufficient *ad rem*. And if I left the matter here, I should have done little to show the bearing of the earlier part of this note upon the present subject. Let me then recall the suggestion that every creature existence is made up of two factors, viz., a definite portion of universal substance, and the arrangement of forces, *i.e.* the body, which marks out and limits that substance. If physical science has established any universal doctrine at all, surely it has established the truth that nothing, whether it be substance or force, is ever annihilated. Neither then of the factors in animal existence can utterly perish. The *forces* which have defined its life return into nature's order, as the distributed type of the printer returns to its fount; but what of the *substance* which these forces isolated from the universe? The view which regards it as "re-merging in the general Soul," has surely a great deal in its favour, although such an opinion needs to be carefully guarded, lest it should degenerate into such a form of Pantheism as denies the Fatherhood of God. But it is surely conceivable, that if the definition and isolation of creature individuality through bodily organization became sufficiently intense, it might survive the shock of death, and henceforward be sustained by more ethereal forces such as would be involved in St. Paul's idea of a celestial body. Here again we have a suggestion given us by the poet, who far more truly than the author of Sartor Resartus, has been the Prophet of his age.

> "Such use may lie in blood and breath:
> Which else were fruitless of their due,
> Had man to learn himself anew
> Beyond the second birth of death."

Supposing such a speculation permissible, then the whole development of the animal creation might be regarded as—to speak humanly—a continued *nisus* to give permanence by definition to finite forms of Universal Substance. Nor—though I do not quote Scripture in *support* of such speculation—can I forbear recalling in connection with such a thought, the words of St. Paul, "*the earnest expectation of the creature waiteth for the manifestation of the sons of God. For the creature was made subject to vanity, not willingly, but by reason of Him who hath subjected the same in hope; because the creature itself also shall be delivered from the bondage of* *corruption into the glorious liberty of the children of God. For we know that the whole creation groaneth and travaileth in pain together until now."\** If then the whole progress of creation has been an effort in the direction of creature immortality, it is not by any means certain that so sharp a line as is sometimes assumed must necessarily be drawn between so-called annihilation and immortality. There is no such thing as annihilation properly so called. The nearest approach to it is absorption into the universe. But it may very fairly be questioned whether anything in the form of created life is ever so completely absorbed into the universe as to become as though it had never existed in that form. The very particles of the decaying body have a power surviving its death, and are richer in influence than they were when previously existing in an inorganic state. And though all scientific knowledge fails us in the attempt to follow the other factor of the creature life, the substance, which is if possible more indestructible than the forces which defined it, we cannot help imagining that it too, after passing through this stage, retains some sort of effect from the process. Where there has been no individuality in mortal life there can be no *individual* immortality; but still, even while absorbed into the life of the universe, the immaterial principle of every beast may enrich or re-enforce that life as its decaying body fertilizes the ground. It is possible to conceive too

\* Rom. viii. 19—22.

that of a number of creatures making different approximations to personality or soul, the function of the immaterial principle in the invisible world of substance may be proportionably various. And only where the isolation has grown defined enough to give a strong sense, or at least a sufficiently determinate germinant sense of individuality and detachment from nature, may the creature life, still marked out and self-conscious, survive the shock of death. The application of such speculations to the development theory will now I hope be obvious. It is not necessary to suppose that the anthropoid predecessors of mankind were all annihilated up to a certain generation, and then suddenly bloomed into immortality. There is no more reason against conceiving various kinds or degrees of immortality, from complete absorption to beatific contemplation, than there is against the acknowledgment of various degrees in the definition of creature existence, from the mere passing bubble of universal life in the barnacle or lichen, to the mysterious microcosm of God and creature, heaven, self and nature in man. As the agitated sea flings its bubbles up into the light, for the most part they do but sparkle a moment and sink again into the bosom of the flood. Some hang together upon the crests of the billows, a mere white streak of foam. But where the ocean is more powerfully moved, the retiring tide often leaves upon the shore wreaths of glassy domes shimmering in the sun with a richness of colour and a perfect symmetry that long survive the struggle of water and air which gave them form.

If we befool ourselves with fancies, the resistless temptation thereto is after all an indication of the strength of that faith which for ever fights with death. If I have stepped beyond the limit of justifiable speculation, it is in protest against the unjustifiable pressure of the dilemma which is too often presented to us,—a faith dependent on contingencies of scientific research, or no faith at all. I repeat I can conceive of no possible contingency which would absolutely exclude immortality. For the rest, the Bible is singularly reserved and certainly encourages no vain curiosity. "*Brethren, we know not what we shall be.*" Happy are we if we realize that divine communion is the power of an endless life; happy if we know that we shall be like Him, because day by day seeing Him, the Divine Humanity, more nearly as He is!

## Note C.

### *On Natural Process and Original Force.*

"No theory which touches the process implies any opinion one way or the other as to the original energy by which the process is worked out." I should have said "the process only," but by an oversight have omitted the latter word. This is the one point upon which in the relations of science and religion all ultimate questions must turn. Yet this is just what extreme men on the one side or the other constantly refuse to see. And it is remarkable how at this point extremes meet. For men who in their superficial zeal for divine creation decline to recognise it in anything but a sudden miraculous act, thereby imply the *absence* of creative energy from all the ordinary processes of the universe. According to them the first pair of each species, and only the first pair, was the product of divine creation; but every successive generation that has come into the world since owes its life entirely and solely to the working of natural laws. At least if this be not their view I am at a loss to understand why they should connect the development theory with atheism. The notion implied is, that wherever the ordinary laws of nature are in operation they are sufficient of themselves to account for everything, and leave no place for God. And thus the extreme advocates of sudden and instantaneous creation agree in the main, whether they know it or not, with the extreme men on the other side, who when they have reduced a number of phenomena to a general law, that is, have defined the *process or mode of operation* observable in all the cases, maintain that no farther explanation is necessary or desirable.

Let us suppose that an intelligent child who had never seen a steam engine, and has no notion of machinery, were on a visit to a manufacturing town, and were told that he should see cotton yarn made by steam. He knows what cotton yarn is; he knows what steam is; but he has no notion of the *process* by which the one is made to produce the other. He has a vague notion however that he is to see them evidently connected together in some surprising and startling manner. But when he is led into the carding room he sees no steam: amongst all the rows of spindles he sees no steam: the self-acting mules do their work like rational creatures, apparently without the slightest assistance from steam. " Why," says the child, " I thought you said the yarn was made by steam; but now you show me how it is made by iron spindles and wheels and straps." " Certainly," answers the guide, " but that is only the process through which the steam works; these are only the tools that steam uses; come to the engine house and I will show you the power that moves it all." Yet even in the engine house, the child would have to take it on faith that inside the cylinder is an invisible vapour which is the secret source of every movement. He would also necessarily have very confused ideas as to the precise links of the mechanical process by which the cotton yarn is produced, ideas which it would require a good many visits to the mill to rectify. But however often his theory on this point required improvement, he need never feel it to affect his original faith as to the motive power of the process.

No doubt the analogy is imperfect. And I should be especially unwilling to countenance the notion that the Creator works upon creation by means of levers and pulleys and cords, which put Him a long way off from it. Nevertheless such an illustration may help plain minds to separate theories as to the process from theories as to the efficient cause.

## Note D.

### *On the Metaphysical Issues of Physical Science.*

In explanation of my meaning in the passing reference to this subject on p. 77, I venture to append an extract from a paper read before the Leicester Literary and Philosophical Society in 1868.

"I wish to say a few words on a third point on which I believe alarmists take a defective view of the facts. I have ventured the remark that they are blind to the metaphysical bearings of the most advanced physical researches. All things have their day in turn, and if we wait long enough their day comes over again. As in the time of Socrates natural history was surrendered for what seemed the more tangible results of metaphysical philosophy; as in more recent times physics have had it all their own way, until philosophy has been almost eager to declare itself materialistic; so now, paradoxical as it may sound to some, I am persuaded we may discern signs that the current will soon turn once again, and that the ultimate issues of all knowledge will be found to land us in immaterial substance and 'the power of an endless life.' The bearing of these remarks may be made clear by a brief reference to some of the most recent speculations on matter and force. The atomic theory of matter is so highly convenient for the purposes of quantitative analysis, that it is often made to assume a delusive appearance of ascertained reality. But I imagine that very few, if any, philosophers of the present day believe in ultimate and indivisible molecules. I used to be told at school that if we had instruments fine enough, we might in process of division come upon these atoms and find they could no longer be divided. Just as a child might break up a conglomeration of pebbles, but could not divide the pebbles themselves, so we were told that if we had the implements we could divide and sub-divide until we reached the little indivisible and indestructible kernels that were called atoms. But since that day one instrument at least has been discovered of a keenness surpassing almost infinitely the subtlest analysis deemed possible in those by-gone days. And not many years ago I listened to a lecture on this discovery, given by an old schoolfellow of mine, who sat once in the same class and learned the same doctrine of atoms, now an eminent Professor of Chemistry. The spectrum analysis was then recent, and has made great progress since that time, but even then enough was shown to manifest an infinite subtlety in the constitution of matter. I remember the line of yellow light, which would intrude when least expected, and the explanation given that sodium is almost everywhere diffused, while the presence of one 80,000th part of a grain will show itself in the spectrum. I remember also a little inch cube of a new metal—cœsium—a substance unknown before the spectrum analysis,—and when told that this minute quantity was the whole result after the evaporation of 40 tons of water, I did not much wonder that it had been hitherto concealed. In the course of the evening, conversing with a great man, too little known and now passed away, I ventured to suggest that this new mode of analysis appeared to refine matter away altogether, and at least to be inconsistent with the theory of ultimate atoms. To this he answered that it only confirmed the view he had held for years,—he had long felt convinced that in the last result matter is nothing but conglomerated centres of force, an opinion which, if I mistake not, is gaining ground, and likely to be universally adopted. If that is the tendency of modern science, to regard all matter as a form of force, then it is a tendency which brings the whole material universe into a closer relationship with our own consciousness of living energy, and at any rate draws it into the field of metaphysical speculation. But force itself has been made the subject of striking experiment and startling hypothesis. And the results have been brought together in Mr. Geo. Grove's treatise on the "Correlation of Forces." The upshot of the whole subject as set forth there is this, that all force is ultimately and essentially one;—that it is in fact a sort of Proteus capable of assuming endless phases, each of which is interchangeable with every other. Thus gravity, or pressure, can be changed into heat,—heat into chemical affinity, this again into electricity, electricity into light, light into organic action,—and on and on through all the modulations of movement in the world. Not only so, but making allowance for dissipation through imperfection of instruments, it is found that each force can be transmuted into an approximate equivalent of its correlative. Thus it is maintained that no force is annihilated, but only changed into equivalents in other forms. The expansive power of the gases in the exploded cannon is not lost or destroyed when the ball falls to the ground. It is only transmuted into a variety of forms, partly into heat, partly into molecular alterations in the metal, partly into currents of air or vibrations through the earth ; and none of these are ever lost, but are diffused, or re-combined, and ever taken up again into the economy of universal energy. For all force is one, though it may show itself in a myriad forms. Now put these two tendencies of physical research together, the disposition to regard all matter as simply a form of force, and all force as ultimately one. What is that One Power by which all things subsist? in which they literally 'live and move and have their being?' It is a question too dread to be hastily answered here. But it does seem to yield a point of view from which all paths of knowledge, like lines of glory on the sea, appear converging towards one issue where we 'lose ourselves in light.' What that issue is of course physical science cannot tell. It owns no speech that can express it, appeals to no faculty that can understand it : but physical science may refine away the coarseness of sense,—it may make the material universe like to a transparent veil which dimly hides the shrine of an Eternal Being,—it may bring us in high wrought tension of soul to the borders of that land where—

> 'on the glimmering limit far withdrawn,
> God makes Himself an awful rose of dawn.'

## Note E.

### *On St. Paul's Revelations.*

In writing to the Galatians (i. 11, 12) St. Paul says. " *I certify you, brethren, that the gospel which was preached of me is not after man. For I neither received it of man, neither was I taught it, but by revelation of Jesus Christ.*" This passage and one or two others of similar import are sometimes insisted on as a stronger proof than even 1 Cor. ii. 13 of St. Paul's claim to be an amanuensis writing from heavenly dictation. But it would be difficult to maintain this. If we except the extraordinary event which produced his conversion, and about which there are differences of opinion, no one contends that St. Paul received his revelations otherwise than in a state of trance or ecstatic vision.* That is, they were instances of pictorial inspiration, and like the visions of the ancient prophets, owed form and colouring to the individuality of the apostle. I can well understand, and to a certain extent sympathize with, the first impulse of a simple faith when confronted with such an assertion, to deny it, and to maintain that in St. Paul's revelations every word was the direct and unrefracted utterance of a Divine Person. But on which side does the burden of proof lie? Surely with that view of the case in hand which is least natural. Now when we hear of visions and trances and dreams it is I hope not presuming too much to say, the *more* natural view is that they must have owed something to the nervous system and imagination and tendencies of the seer; while the *least* natural view is that such human elements had no part in the matter. I am assuming all through, that such visions and trances were a possible medium of inspiration. Whether they were actually so must be determined by the results; and in St. Paul's case these are amply sufficient to determine it in the affirmative. But a medium of inspiration is one thing, and direct heavenly dictation is another. And as I have suggested,

---

\* Acts xxii. 17. 2 Cor. xii. 2. St. Paul seems also to have been occasionally directed by dreams. Acts xvi. 9; xxvii. 23.

the burden of proof lies with those who maintain the latter in the present case. But how will they set about it? So far as St. Paul gives any description of his state of mind under "the abundance of revelations," his words rather confirm the more natural view than otherwise. In recalling one of the most remarkable of such experiences he says that whether he was at the time in the body or out of the body he cannot tell.\* A fortiori then he would be incapable of determining whether the "unspeakable words" were heard outwardly or inwardly; whether they were entirely independent of his own subjectivity or not. On what then can those who adhere to the less natural view rely? St. Paul says that he received certain things by revelation from heaven—*what things* we shall presently try to determine. We fully admit the reality and divine source of these revelations: but we maintain that they came in the form of pictorial inspiration, and form no exception to the usual mingling of heavenly suggestions with human thoughts. If asked why we believe the suggestions to have been from heaven; we answer, because of their fruits, because of their power over the God-consciousness in humanity. If asked why we believe these suggestions to have become mingled with mistakes natural to the time, or to have been developed only imperfectly in some respects; we answer, because those suggestions, however bright, left St Paul at liberty to argue occasionally like

\* 2 Cor. xii. 1—4. That "of" possesses St. Paul describes his own experience is, as Dean Alford remarks, evident from v. 7.

a Rabbi,* and to import meanings into the Old Testament, which, with all our veneration for his authority, it is impossible for us to receive as really belonging to it :† because also his ideas about the near approach of Christ's second coming,‡ besides his constant adoption of current ideas about the unseen world,§ show that while the abundance of the revelations gave him an extraordinary elevation of spiritual life, it did not give him any clear information as to the real bearing of Christ's mission on the future, that is, its place in history. But what reasons for their belief can be adduced by those who maintain that our Lord himself, or his angel, revealed the truth to St. Paul in articulately spoken language infallibly distinguishable from his own thoughts? Putting aside the manifestations of Christ in Acts ix, in which so far as we know nothing new was revealed, the *only* reason for such a supposition in regard to any of the revelations is the alleged confidence and assertion of St. Paul that so it was. But where is the assertion? To produce the above passage from Galatians (i. 11, 12) is simply to beg the question. I have shown that it is susceptible of two different interpretations, of which one is more, and the other less natural. The reason for adopting the less natural interpretation must surely be something outside the passage itself. It may be said that in 1 Cor. xi. 23 the apostle distinctly declares that he received by

---

\* *e.g.* Gal. iii. 16   † *e.g.* Acts xiii. 34—37.
‡ 1 Thess. iv. 15—17 ; 2 Thess. ii. 6, 9.   § 2 Cor. xii. 2 ; Eph. vi. 12.

revelation a fact of gospel history. But is it at all credible that even Saul the persecutor was ignorant of the Christian custom of the Eucharist, or of the account given of it by the disciples? The above passage must necessarily be interpreted in one of two modes, neither of which is opposed to the views here suggested on St. Paul's revelations. Either it means " I have received and delivered to you the sacred tradition which originated with the Lord himself;" or it means that a fact which the apostle already knew beforehand was sanctified and raised to a higher significance by the revelations with which he was favoured. There is in truth no assertion of the apostle's to be found, which is at all inconsistent with the idea that his revelations were, like prophetic visions, ordinary inspiration in a pictorial form.

Notwithstanding, however, the absence of any assertion which involves it, let us suppose that St. Paul, by his general mode of speech, suggests a confidence on his part that his revelations were something essentially distinct from his ordinary inspiration, an assurance that unlike the latter, the former consisted in direct, articulate, infallible communications of unmingled truth. That his confidence is of such a nature as would justify the inference of which I have spoken above, I do not for a moment allow. To make such an inference legitimate, we ought to have some good ground for believing that the apostle was in the habit of distinguishing between the divine suggestions that kindled his soul on the one hand, and the forms of thought natural to his own individual character on the other; also that in his revelations he arrived deliberately at the conclusion, that his own mind and heart had nothing whatever to do with the nature of the impressions he received. But no such indications exist.* On the contrary, in his most exalted trance he could not even tell whether he was in the body or out of it; and in giving advice on a subject concerning which no decisive external authority could be quoted, he says, "*I think also for my part that I have the spirit of God.*"† Still, for the sake of a farther point to which I would call attention, let it be allowed that the apostle was morally confident of the unmingled purity of the communications made to him in his visions. On what, then, did his confidence rest? In answering this question it is often quietly assumed that St. Paul realized the visit of an angel or a spirit in the same way in which we realize the entrance of a friend into our chamber, and that the communications of such visitants were made in an equally objective manner. But it need hardly be said that with the exception of the appearance of the risen Lord described in Acts ix., an appearance which is usually regarded as something more than spiritual, there is no ground whatever for such an assumption. The eyes and ears, so far as they were concerned at all, were acted on not from without but from within; and St. Paul's confidence

---

\* 1 Cor. vii. 10—12 has quite a different bearing; on which see Lecture iii. p. 95.

† δοκῶ δὲ κἀγὼ πνεῦμα θεοῦ ἔχειν 1 Cor. vii. 40.

in such cases as his trance in the Temple\* and the answer to his prayer for deliverance from the thorn in the flesh,† could not possibly depend on the evidence of his senses. On what then did it depend? He himself believed that Satan might possibly appear as an angel of light.‡ He was looking for the revelation of " that Wicked . . whose coming is after the working of Satan, with all power and signs and lying wonders." Therefore he could not think that the miraculous nature of his visions was in itself any infallible guarantee of their unmingled divinity;§ and the extraordinary character of his experience could not be the ultimate foundation of his confidence. Then what was that foundation? We answer it was a moral and spiritual understanding of what was congruous with the majesty of God. *"God who commanded the light to shine out of darkness hath shined in our hearts to give the light of the knowledge of the glory of God in the face of Jesus Christ."*∥ *"Now he that hath wrought us for the self-same thing is God, who also hath given unto us the earnest of the spirit. Therefore we are always confident."*¶ *"He that is spiritual judgeth all things, yet he himself is judged of no man. For who hath known the mind of the Lord, that he may instruct him? But we have the mind of Christ."*\*\*

\* Acts xxii. 17.  † 2 Cor. xii. 8, 9.
‡ 2 Cor. xi. 14.   § Comp. 1 John iv. 1—3.
∥ 2 Cor. iv. 6.    ¶ 2 Cor. v. 5, 6.

\*\* 1 Cor. ii. 15, 16, *νοῦν i.e.* the reason, purpose, or—speaking reverently—cast of thought.' The idea is that having the mind of Christ formed within us, we are able to discern the mind of God.

But if St. Paul's own confidence in the revelations vouchsafed to him was moral, not positive; subjective, not objective; the perception of a divine glory, not blind submission to portents; does it not follow that any confidence which he generates in us must be of the same kind? The difference between this kind of confidence and that which by an abuse of the passage in Galatians (i. 11, 12) is demanded from us is plain. When St. Paul says concerning the risen Lord: "*last of all he was seen of me also;*" every one who believes the apostle to have been an honest man and to have uttered these words, takes his word for the fact, however it may be explained. We may not understand the precise nature of the manifestation, nor even try to explain it. All we know is that the form of the Lord Jesus was made visible to him, and we take his word for that. In this we allow him the authority which belongs to every honest witness who testifies of a matter which he alone knows. There is not necessarily required any sympathy with him, or agreement with his opinions. All that such authority touches is the bare fact. Similarly when St. Paul speaks of his visions and revelations in a state of trance; we believe that he had such experiences simply on his authority. But when we are commanded on this account to receive as infallible truth every word he uttered, we ask how he distinguished heavenly suggestions from spiritual delusions or national and individual peculiarities? As we have seen, the only possible answer is that he did so by spiritual discernment, a gift in which he insists that all Christians ought to share. Here, then, the simple and direct action of authority is out of place. So far as we really and heartily accept his revelations we can only do so because we, like him, feel that they are congruous with "the glory of God in the face of Jesus Christ." This is the only acceptance that he cared for when on earth. And could he now speak from heaven he would not depart from the spirit in which he wrote to the Philippians, "*if in anything ye be otherwise minded, God shall reveal even this unto you; nevertheless whereto we have already attained let us walk by the same rule, let us mind the same thing.*"

In conclusion let me say, what ought perhaps to have been said before, that the inferences from Gal. i. 11, 12, on which I have commented, are obviously founded on a total misunderstanding of the passage. For the sake of the argument, and to allow such inferences the strongest conceivable ground, I have spoken as though I accepted the interpretation. But to any one who considers that the *young man Saul* was no stranger in Jerusalem, and that he had a persecutor's interest in making himself acquainted with everything in Christianity which was repulsive to the Jews, that is, with all the salient points of its history and doctrine, it will be perfectly plain that St. Paul did not and could not mean to tell the Galatians that he had received from heaven his information of Christian facts. What then did he mean? In chap. ii. 2 he tells us that in visiting Jerusalem he communicated to the other apostles "that gospel" which he preached among the Gentiles. Now certainly he did not declare among the Gentiles any other facts than those preached at Jerusalem. What he means then by "that gospel" is that aspect of saving truth in its freedom from Mosaism, which was specially adapted to the Gentiles, and which he was divinely commissioned to preach to them. But whatever is meant by "that gospel" in chap. ii. is certainly also signified by "the gospel which was preached of me," (i. 11). And when he says that he "neither received it of man, neither was taught it, but by revelation of Jesus Christ," he clearly means that the free non-Mosaic Gospel which he proclaimed came to him when he was in Arabia or Damascus, in solitary communion with the Spirit of the Lord Jesus; while he maintains that his commission to declare it was quite as divine as that of Peter and James to preach a gospel suited to the circumcision. Farther, as St. Paul deeply felt how essential to the yet undeveloped glory of " the ministration of the Spirit" was this freedom from the letter, we can well understand the vehemence with which he denounced those who would have entangled the Galatians again in the yoke of bondage. On this—certainly the more reasonable—interpretation of the passage, its entire agreement with the purport of this note needs no farther remark.

## Note F.

### *Eusebius on the Canon.*

To readers not well acquainted with the range of testimony on which the existing Canon of the New Testament depends, it might appear that what I have said on p. 113 about Eusebius is scarcely consistent with what is afterwards asserted on p. 134 concerning the Christian Scriptures. But let us distinguish clearly between two conceivable views of the New Testament, and the consistency of the two passages will I hope be clear. One view then tends to regard the Canon as a standard clearly, nay even miraculously defined, from the time when the latest book now found in it was completed; and as containing the only law of the Church, from the death of the last of the Apostles. According to this view, Christian tradition and opinion ought always to have been ruled by the Canon, and never the Canon by tradition or opinion. Against such an idea the words of Eusebius alone are a very serious and even fatal objection. Another view holds that the books of the Canon were gradually separated from a number of others through the operation of Christian tradition and opinion, *i.e.* the voice of the Church; and were honoured in proportion to the increasing reverence felt for their apostolic or quasi-apostolic authors. On this view the Canon may have remained comparatively unsettled for centuries without any general doubt being necessarily thrown on the authorship of the collection: and at the same time the question which should have most interest for us is not so much what authority belongs to the Canon as a whole, but rather what evidence is there for the authorship of the different books? This is the view which is implied in the present Lectures.

Premising these remarks, let me sum up the testimony of Eusebius,* and its bearing. Amongst the acknowledged books he places the four Gospels, the Acts, the fourteen—or to speak more exactly—thirteen epistles of St. Paul, (mentioning a doubt only about that to the Hebrews,†) the first Epistles of Peter and of John. In the second class, or those doubtful, he places (the Epistle to the Hebrews,) the second of Peter, those of James, and Jude, and the second and third of John. About the Apocalypse he hesitates considerably: indeed the classification is altogether somewhat uncertain; but after mentioning the Revelation doubtfully in the two former classes he seems finally inclined to resign it to the third, or that of the rejected and spurious.

Such a passage serves very well to illustrate what has been said about the mode of regarding the scriptures in early Christian times. So far as it goes however it confirms our belief in the apostolic authorship of the

---

\* H. E. iii. 3, 24, 25.

† ὅτι γε μὴν τινὲς ἠθετήκασι τὴν πρὸς Ἑβραίους πρὸς τῆς Ῥωμαίων ἐκ κλησίας ὡς μὴ Παύλου οὖσαν αὐτὴν ἀντιλέγεσθαι φήσαντες οὐ δίκαιον ἀγνοεῖν. "That however some have rejected the (Epistle) to the Hebrews, and have alleged an objection to it on the part of the Roman Church, as not being written by Paul, it were not right to ignore."—H. E. iii. 2.

majority of the books. And as to the one which he seems disposed to reject, viz., the Revelation of St. John, it is in our times precisely the comparative certainty of its authorship which is urged on many hands as an objection to the Johannine origin of the fourth Gospel. The two books, it is said, are so different that they could not have been written by the same man; and we have much more evidence for the authorship of the Apocalypse than for that of the Gospel. I do not agree in these assertions, particularly the last. I only adduce them now to show that a doubt cast upon a book in one or more early writers is not necessarily a very strong argument against it. Though perhaps nine-tenths or even more of the literature existing in the time of Eusebius has been destroyed, yet through the advance of scholarship modern critics are able to make a much better use of what remains, than he could make of all the libraries at his service. And so it comes to pass that earlier references which he ignored or slighted are wrought out now into clear and trustworthy evidence. Justin Martyr, writing in the middle of the second century gives what is now considered unimpeachable testimony in favour of the Apocalypse; and though perhaps some of us might be glad to sacrifice it if we might thereby secure the fourth Gospel for St. John clear of all controversy, such a course is not open to us. It should be remembered however that the same Justin has some pretty clear reminiscences of St. John's Gospel; that Papias appears to take from it his list of

Apostles whose testimony he loves to hear from surviving elders;* and that if the quotations in Hippolytus are to be trusted, the gospel was referred to in favour of their opinions by the earliest Gnostics of the second century.

These illustrations may suggest to hasty readers the danger of any too rash conclusions about New Testament books from the doubts or the silence of early ecclesiastical writers. When once the notion of Biblical infallibility is universally and frankly surrendered, I am persuaded that not only will the real inspiration of the sacred writers be more genuinely appreciated, but the question of authorship will be discussed with less of passion and prejudice, and as I believe with the result of establishing substantially the ecclesiastical tradition on which the present Canon is founded.

* Andrew, Peter, Philip, Thomas, James, John, Matthew. See a masterly article by Steitz in Studien und Kritiken, 1868, Heft iii. Die Tradition von der Wirksamkeit des Apostels Johannes in Ephesus. He urges with great force that leaving out Matthew, whose presence he accounts for by the fact of his being the only other evangelist among the Apostles, the remaining six appear precisely in the order in which they occur in St. John's narrative, an order entirely different from the classified lists in the synoptic gospels, with which alone it is said that Papias was acquainted. The two sons of Zebedee come last in the list, though among the greatest. But if the writer was running over in his mind the names of the Apostles as they occur in St. John's Gospel, this is natural; for they are not distinctly mentioned till the last chapter. When it is remembered that John alone gives a character and a voice to three of the above mentioned, Andrew, Philip, and Thomas; when it is borne in mind that with the dubious exception of Nathanael, Papias mentions *all* the Apostles appearing in St. John, and *precisely in the order in which they appear*, it will perhaps be acknowledged that a more acute and discerning and suggestive critical observation has rarely been made than this of Steitz on the well worn passage of Papias.

## Note G.

### *On the Divinity of Christ.*

In reference to the assumption of our Lord's earthly omniscience I have not noticed the practically Cerinthian theory which I suppose some would regard as satisfactory, I mean the notion that *qua* divine he was omniscient, but *qua* human he was not. I have not noticed it because, however stated, it is to me simply a collection of articulate sounds without any meaning whatever. The nearest approach I can make to the attachment of any meaning to it is this, that the Divine and the Human were in Christ so distinct, that the one could know what the other did not and could hide that meaning from the other. But such a separation is evidently inconsistent with any genuine unity of person. For it would amount to the proposition that the same Person knew and did *not* know the same thing, in the same sense, at the same moment.

If any one prefers to think that omniscience was *latent* in the veiled divinity of the Lord, and only came to the surface of consciousness according to the needs of the hour, *that* view is perfectly consistent with all that is advanced on this subject in Lecture V. The needs of the hour did not require that the\* Son should know the time for the end of the world, and much less

\* Mark x. 32.

did they require that the Messiah should know the time when the Jewish canon began or closed.

The only vital interest which such a question can have for ordinary Christians who are content with the practical power of godliness, arises from the supposed relation of the subject to the divinity of Christ. This is of course much too large an issue to enter upon here. I only desire to record my conviction that the question does not at all necessarily affect the reality or essentiality of the divinity of the Lord. Whatever be the original mystery of Christ's person (as to which, probably a deeper philosophy of creation is needed before we get even the right point of view), we all believe that in respect to that mystery he emptied or impoverished himself*, and "was found in fashion as a man." The more the correlation of limitation in knowledge with all other limitations of humanity is considered, the more will it be felt that this "emptying" or impoverishment must have included the former. And if a consciously divine life could not be limited in that way, then the incarnation or manifestation of God in humanity is impossible, because a contradiction in terms. But any one, who has reflected upon the multifarious divine self-limitations involved in Creation, will I am persuaded find no insuperable difficulty at all in the notion of a Being consciously consubstantial with God, yet limited in knowledge.

* Phil. ii. 7. ἐκένωσεν ἑαυτόν

After all, the aspects in which the divinity of Christ most directly and practically affects our religious life are his intense unrivalled consciousness of God, and his oneness in feeling, disposition and will with the heavenly Father. By the first he raised our abject and despairing human life into the pleroma of the Divine Love; by the second he assures us that in his sympathy, purity and self-sacrifice we have a true expression of God's purpose towards the world. Though it is doubtless true that we are embraced by God's everlasting arms even when we least know it, yet it is also true that the purifying influence of His love can only be realized in proportion as we are consciously its objects. And this is what Christ makes us to be by the light which his intense *consciousness of God* shed upon the *God-consciousness* in man. Through his infinitely strong and clear perception of God as Subject no less than Object, together with his marvellous power to propagate this sense in others, we come to have a feeling quite as comprehensive and far more elevating than the Nature-worship of the Greeks, the feeling of a Divinity underlying, pervading, over-ruling, glorifying all things. Again, the assurance that we have "the knowledge of the glory of God in the face of Jesus Christ," that the Lord's moral nature and spiritual ministry are an expression of God's will towards the world, or in other words of the Final Cause of creation,—this it is which satisfies the heart and quickens in the soul that faith which practically justifies by giving an adequate end in life. These two aspects of Christ's Being, his supreme consciousness of God, and that unity with the Father which is inconceivable apart from consubstantiality, make every word and deed of the Lord Jesus luminous with suggestive revelations of the divine background of existence, and confer an infinite preciousness upon His endurance and death, as an embodiment of the true relations between sinful man and God's loving unrevengeful goodness. I believe that these two aspects of the Lord's divine humanity are the one source of all peculiarly evangelical power and fervour, from St. Paul's epistles, or the truly inspired letter to Diognetus, down to John Wesley, or the Ritualists and the Primitive Methodists, who at opposite poles are Wesley's true successors. No revolutions of thought which leave any sort of practical reality to these aspects of Christ's Being will in the slightest degree imperil "the power of God unto salvation," which Christianity enshrines. Nor do I think that this vital essence of the Old Faith is even seriously threatened. Some one may ask, "is it possible you can be so blind as to suppose that the dogma of a Man's divinity is likely to survive the reduction of human nature to protoplasm?" If you mean the dogma of the Athanasian creed, I answer, No. But if you mean the direct intuitive consciousness of Christ that his deepest self was God, and his humanity a transparency through which God shone, I say, Yes. This transition period is but a sort of "blind man's holiday," and the blind often make a far better use of their other senses than do the keen-sighted. I may be blind, but I have a strong *feeling* that the divinity which has made Christ the Lord of modern history is losing none of its significance. The gospel of protoplasm is very far from being opposed to the Gospel of God.

> " Not only cunning casts in clay !
> Let science prove we are and then."—

But science cannot do it. The really prophetic signs of the times point in a very different, indeed an opposite direction.

# TITLES OF SOME USEFUL BOOKS ON HISTORICAL THEOLOGY, BIBLICAL CRITICISM, MORAL PHILOSOPHY, &c. PUBLISHED BY WILLIAMS AND NORGATE.

*Sent Post free for the published price.*

Apocryphal Gospels, and other Documents relating to the History of Christ. Translated from the Originals in Greek, Latin, Syriac, &c., with Notes, References, and Prolegomena. By B. HARRIS COWPER. 3rd Edition. 8vo., cloth  6s.

Bible (The) Considered as a Record of Historical Development. 8vo., sewed  1s.

Campbell (Douglas) New Religious Thoughts. A Second Edition, with considerable alterations. Crown 8vo., cloth  5s.

Davidson (Dr. S.) An Introduction to the Old Testament, critical, historical, and theological, containing a discussion of the most important questions belonging to the several Books. By SAMUEL DAVIDSON, D.D., LL.D. 3 vols. 8vo., cloth  42s.

Donaldson (Rev. Dr.) Christian Orthodoxy reconciled with the conclusions of modern Biblical learning. A Theological Essay, with critical and controversial Supplements. 8vo. (pub. at 10s.)  6s.

Fellowes (Robert, LL.D.) The Religion of the Universe, with consolatory Views of a Future State, and suggestions on the most beneficial topics of Theological Instruction. 3rd Edition. Post 8vo., cloth  6s.

14, Henrietta Street, Covent Garden, London.

# WILLIAMS AND NORGATE'S

### Free Christian Union Publications.

1. Sidgwick (H.) The Ethics of Conformity and Subscription. By Henry Sidgwick M.A. late Fellow of Trinity College, Cambridge. 1s.
2. Two Sermons. By Athanase Coquerel Fils, and the Rev. C. Kegan Paul, M.A. Preached at the First Anniversary of the Free Christian Union 1s.
3. Martineau (Rev. J.) The New Affinities of Faith. A plea for Free Christian Union 1s.
4. Tayler (Rev. J. J.) Christianity: What is It? and What has it Done? 1s.
5. Tayler (Rev. J. J.) A Catholic Christian Church the Want of our Time. 1s.

**Genesis of the Earth and of Man**; or, a History of Creation and the Antiquity of Races of Mankind: a critical Examination of passages in the Hebrew and Greek Scriptures, relating to Questions of Geology and Ethnology. Edited by R. S. POOLE. Second Edition, revised and enlarged. Crown 8vo. cloth 6s.

**Goodsir (J. T.) The Westminster Confession of Faith**, Examined on the Basis of the other Protestant Confessions. 8vo., cloth 10s. 6d.

**Goodsir (J. T.) The Biblical and Patristic Doctrine of Salvation**, and other Papers. 2 vols. 8vo., cloth 15s.

**Griffith (Rev. D.) The Continuity of Religious Development.** By the Rev. DAVID GRIFFITH. Seven Sermons; with an Appendix of Notes. 8vo. cloth 6s.

**Infinite Love: a Meditation.** By ΕΥΒΟΥΛΟΣ ΒΑΣΑΝΙΣΤΗΣ. "God is love." Crown 8vo. 1s.

**Janet (Paul) The Materialism of the Present Day.** A Critique on Dr. Büchner's System. By PAUL JANET, Member of the Institute of France, Professor of Philosophy at the Paris Faculté des Lettres. Translated by GUSTAVE MASSON, B.A. Crown 8vo., cloth 3s.

**The Jesus of History.** 8vo., cloth 12s.

**King (E. M.) Truth, Love, Joy**; or, the Garden of Eden and its Fruits. Post 8vo., cloth. (Melbourne, Victoria.) 8s. 6d.

**Kirkus (Rev. W.) Orthodoxy, Scripture and Reason**: an Examination of some of the principal Articles of Creed of Christendom. Crown 8vo., cloth 10s. 6d.

*11, Henrietta Street, Covent Garden, London.*

## PUBLICATIONS.

**Lloyd (W. Watkiss) Christianity in the Cartoons,** referred to artistic treatment and historic fact. Illustrated with 12 photographs and 4 plates. 8vo., cloth  21s.

**Lowndes (Richard) on the Philosophy of Primary Beliefs.** Crown 8vo., cloth  7s. 6d.

**Mackay (R. W.) The Tübingen School and its Antecedents.** A Review of the History and present Condition of Modern Theology. 8vo., cloth  10s. 6d.

**Mackay (R. W.) Progress of the Intellect,** as exemplified in the Religious Development of the Greeks and Hebrews. 2 vols. 8vo., cloth (pub. at 24s.)  21s.

**Mackay (R. W.) Sketch of the Rise and Progress of Christianity.** 8vo. cloth (pub. at 10s. 6d.)  6s.

**Mackay (R. W.) The Sophistes of Plato:** a Dialogue on True and False Teaching. Translated with explanatory Notes, and an Introduction of Ancient and Modern Sophistry. Crown 8vo., cloth  5s.

**Mackay (R. W.) Christian Perfectibility.** The Eternal Gospel; or, the Idea of Christian Perfectibility. Crown 8vo., cloth  3s.

**Man's (A) Belief:** an Essay on the Facts of Religious Knowledge. Crown 8vo., sewed  2s.

**Martineau (Rev. Jas.) A Word for Scientific Theology,** in appeal from the Men of Science and the Theologians. 8vo., sewed, 1s.

**Neale (E. Vansittart, M.A.) The Analogy of Thought and Nature investigated.** 8vo., cloth  7s. 6d.

**Parry, Christianity versus Theology.** In Ten Letters, addressed to his brother Laymen. By WILLIAM PARRY, an Octogenarian Layman of the Church of England. Crown 8vo. 2s.

**Quarry (Rev. J.) Genesis and its Authorship.** Two Dissertations. 1. On the Import of the Introductory Chapters of the Book of Genesis. 2. On the Use of the Names of God in the Book of Genesis, and on the Unity of its Authorship. By the Rev. J. QUARRY, M.A., Rector of Midleton, Cork, Prebendary of Cloyne. 650 pp. 8vo., cloth  18s.

20, South Frederic Street, Edinburgh.

Shore (Rev. Th.) The Churchman and the Free Thinker; or a Friendly Address to the Orthodox. 8vo., cloth  2s. 6d.

Spencer (Herbert) First Principles. Second Edition, re-organized and further developed. 8vo., cloth  16s.

Spencer (Herbert) The Principles of Biology. 2 vols. 8vo. cloth  34s.

Spencer (Herbert) The Principles of Psychology. A new Edition in the Press.

Spencer (Herbert) Education: Intellectual, Moral, and Physical. 8vo., cloth  6s.

Spencer (Herbert) Social Statics; or, the Conditions essential to Human Happiness specified, and the First of them developed. Cheaper Edition. 8vo., cloth  10s.

Spencer (Herbert) Essays: Scientific, Political, and Speculative. (Being the First and Second Series re-arranged, and containing an additional Essay.) Cheaper Edition. 2 vols. 8vo., cloth  16s.

Stark (J.) On the Inspiration of the Scriptures, showing the Testimony which they themselves bear as to their own Inspiration. By JAMES STARK, M.D. Crown 8vo., cloth  3s. 6d.

Strauss (Dr. D. F.) New Life of Jesus. The Authorized English Edition. 2 vols. 8vo., cloth  24s.

Tayler (Rev. J. J.) An attempt to ascertain the Character of the Fourth Gospel, especially in its relation to the three First. New Edition. 8vo., cloth  5s.

Theological Review: A Journal of Religious Thought and Life. Published Quarterly. Each No. 8vo.  2s. 6d. Nos. 1 to 11 each 2s.—Nos. 12 to 30 each 2s. 6d.—No. XXX., July, 1870.

Williams (Dr. Rowland) The Prophets of Israel and Judah during the Assyrian Empire. Translated afresh, and Illustrated for English readers. 8vo., cloth  10s. 6d.

Williams (Dr. Rowland) Broadchalke Sermon-Essays, on Nature, Mediation, Atonement, Absolution, &c. Crown 8vo. 7s. 6d.

www.ingramcontent.com/pod-product-compliance
Lightning Source LLC
Chambersburg PA
CBHW031752230426
43669CB00007B/585